Copyright ©   1989 by NECEF
First edition   1988
Second edition 1989

ISBN 0-937807-11-7

Palestine and the Palestinians

A Handbook

Produced By The Near East Cultural and Educational Foundation of Canada

WITH OUR THANKS

NECEF is grateful to the authors who volunteered their time, expertise and papers in preparing the text. We especially appreciate the work of Dr. Farid Ohan who designed the cover, prepared the plates and organized the volunteers to collate the pages. We also want to thank Mr. Bassam Sharif of Discount Printing, for allowing us to use his printing facilities. We want to thank the Information Office of the League of Arab States in Ottawa for a grant which helped cover the costs of printing this edition of _Palestine and the Palestinians_.

TABLE OF CONTENTS

INTRODUCTION

What is the Palestinian-Israeli question and why should we be interested in it in 1988?

Two peoples have struggled since the beginning of the twentieth century for control of Palestine. The Palestinian Arabs have sought to remain in or regain the only homeland they have known; the Jews, originally mainly European, have sought to create a homeland, indeed a state, for Jews from Europe and the rest of the world, in the Palestinians' land.

The conflict has involved neighbouring Arab states like Egypt, Jordan, Syria and Lebanon, some or all of them in five short but bitter wars with Israel. Great imperial powers like France, Britain and the U.S.A. have participated over the years as allies, occupiers, aggressors or arms suppliers. To understand this continuing conflict, probably the most complex in present-day world affairs, we must examine such issues as the following:

1. the right of Palestinians to their own homes on land held for more than a thousand years.
2. the right of Palestinians to sovereignty in their own state.
3. the Jews' demand for a state of their own as a haven from the discrimination and persecution from which they suffered for centuries in Europe and elsewhere.
4. the Zionist claim that the Jews possess exclusive sovereignty over Palestine on the basis of divine promises to their forefathers, the Patriarchs, as recorded in the Old Testament. Through the centuries the Jews have maintained their religious and cultural attachment to their Holy Land.
5. the creation of Israel as an exclusively Jewish state.
6. the contentious issue of sacred sites. Since Jerusalem is a holy city to three faiths -- Judaism, Islam and Christianity; since Jerusalem is the third most sacred city to Muslims (after Mecca and Medina) and 90 percent of all Arabs are Muslims; and since two very sacred mosques, the Dome of the Rock and al-Aqsa, are built on the site of the former Jewish temple, the possibility for violent clashes is ever present.
7. the anger of the Arabs at the founding of an "alien" Jewish state with the support of imperial powers like France, Britain and now the United States.

i

8. the intrusion of Cold War rivalries, the United States and the Soviet Union, both fearing the interference of the other with their interests in the region, interests such as oil or supplying weapons.
9. the proliferation of nuclear weapons. Both Israel and Pakistan (a Muslim country) possess nuclear arms, posing a dangerous threat to the peoples of the Middle East and indeed to the rest of the world, especially in view of the Cold War.
10. the role of countries like Canada. Canadians bear some responsibility because in 1947 Canada supported the partition of Palestine, in 1956 and afterwards took part in the United Nations peace-keeping team, and today are concerned about war, economic interests and human rights.

MANDATED PALESTINE 1920-1948

(Area: 10,435 square miles)

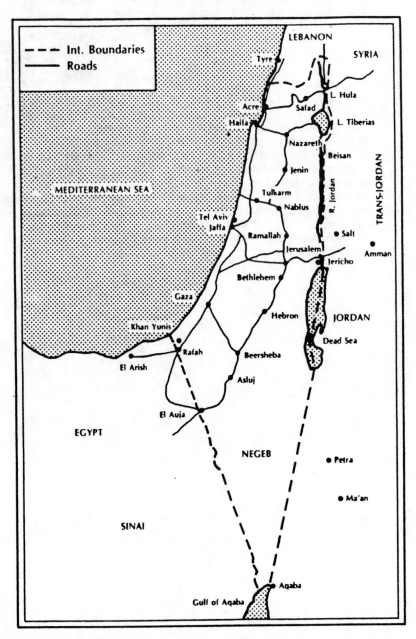

Provided By Sami Hadawi.

ZIONIST PROPOSALS FOR A "ZIONIST STATE"
(As submitted to the Paris Peace Conference, 1919)

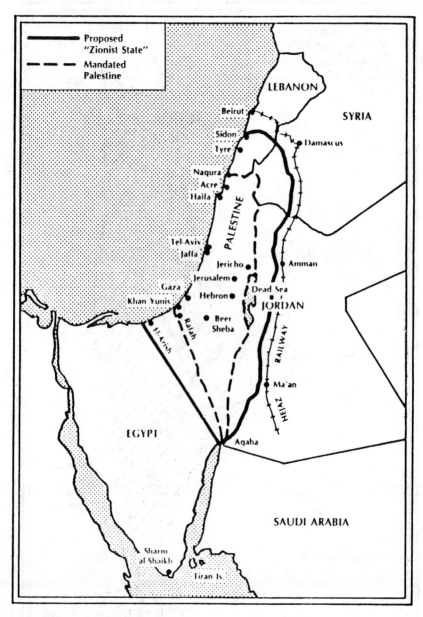

Provided By Sami Hadawi

iv

PARTITION PLAN, 1947

(U.N. Resolution 181 (II), November 29, 1947

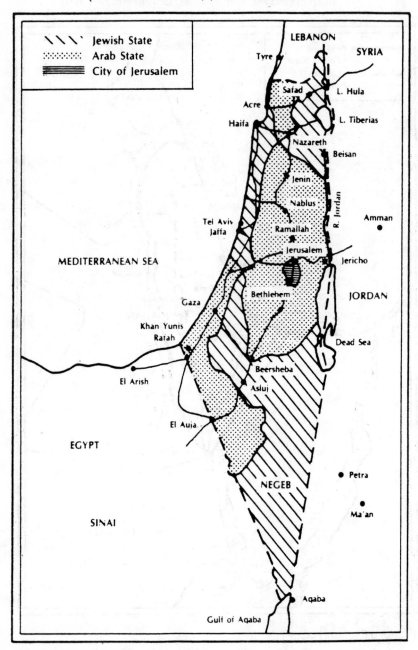

ARMISTICE AGREEMENT, 1949

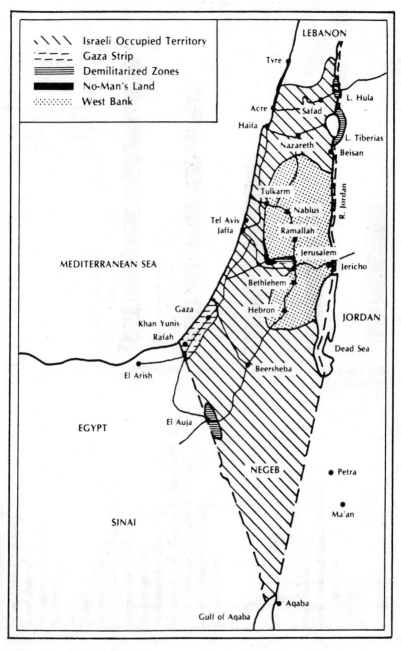

Provided By Sami Hadawi

POPULATION AND IMMIGRATION CHARTS

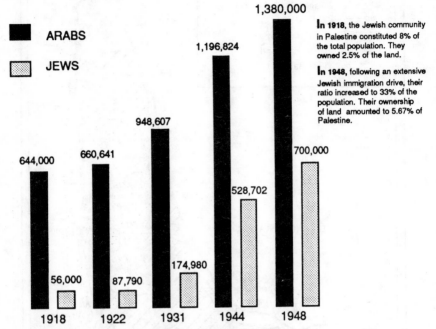

ARABS

JEWS

1,380,000

In **1918**, the Jewish community in Palestine constituted 8% of the total population. They owned 2.5% of the land.

In **1948**, following an extensive Jewish immigration drive, their ratio increased to 33% of the population. Their ownership of land amounted to 5.67% of Palestine.

1,196,824

948,607

700,000

644,000   660,641   528,702

174,980

56,000   87,790

1918   1922   1931   1944   1948

THE ARAB POPULATION AND THE JEWISH MINORITY
1918-1948

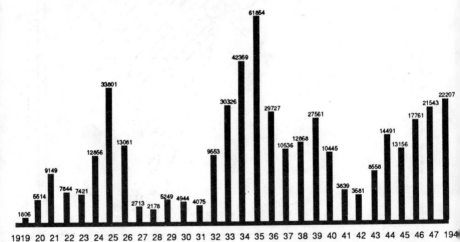

JEWISH IMMIGRATION DRIVES INTO PALESTINE (1918-1948)
(Figures are as reported in the British Official Records. These figures do not include clandistine immigration).

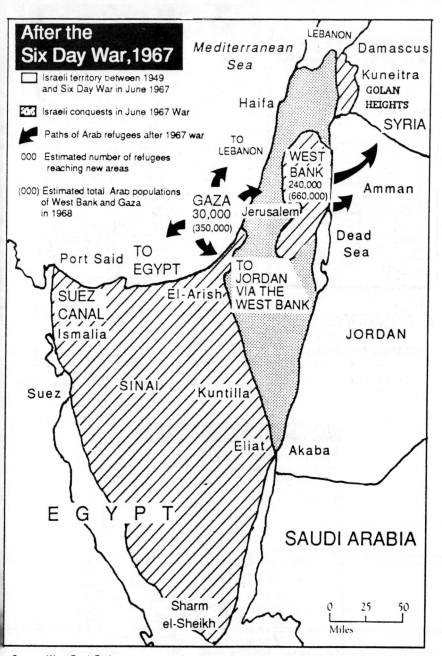

After the Six Day War, 1967

- ☐ Israeli territory between 1949 and Six Day War in June 1967
- ▨ Israeli conquests in June 1967 War
- ◤ Paths of Arab refugees after 1967 war
- 000 Estimated number of refugees reaching new areas
- (000) Estimated total Arab populations of West Bank and Gaza in 1968

LEBANON

Mediterranean Sea

Damascus

Kuneitra
GOLAN HEIGHTS

Haifa

SYRIA

TO LEBANON

WEST BANK
240,000
(660,000)

Amman

GAZA
30,000
(350,000)

Jerusalem

Dead Sea

Port Said

TO EGYPT

El-Arish

TO JORDAN VIA THE WEST BANK

JORDAN

SUEZ CANAL

Ismalia

Suez

SINAI

Kuntilla

EGYPT

Eliat

Akaba

SAUDI ARABIA

Sharm el-Sheikh

0   25   50
Miles

Source: West Bank Project.
(West Bank population figures do not include East Jerusalem.

viii

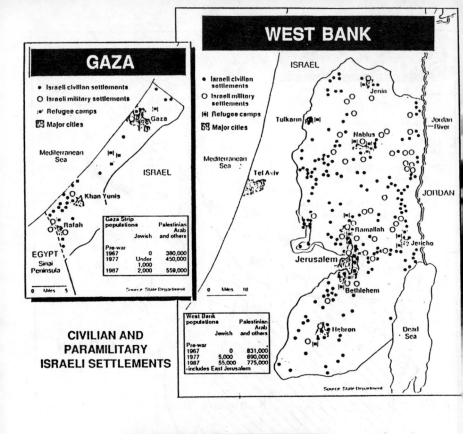

GAZA

- Israeli civilian settlements
- ○ Israeli military settlements
- ▣ Refugee camps
- ▩ Major cities

Mediterranean Sea

ISRAEL

Khan Yunis

Rafah

EGYPT
Sinai Peninsula

Gaza Strip populations		Palestinian Arab and others
	Jewish	
Pre-war		
1967	0	380,000
1977	Under 1,000	450,000
1987	2,000	559,000

Source: State Department

0 Miles 5

CIVILIAN AND PARAMILITARY ISRAELI SETTLEMENTS

WEST BANK

ISRAEL

- Israeli civilian settlements
- ○ Israeli military settlements
- ▣ Refugee camps
- ▩ Major cities

Mediterranean Sea

Tel Aviv

Jenin

Tulkarm

Nablus

Jordan River

JORDAN

Ramallah

Jericho

Jerusalem

Bethlehem

Hebron

Dead Sea

West Bank populations		Palestinian Arab and others
	Jewish	
Pre-war		
1967	0	831,000
1977	5,000	690,000
1987	55,000	775,000

*includes East Jerusalem

0 Miles 10

Source: State Department

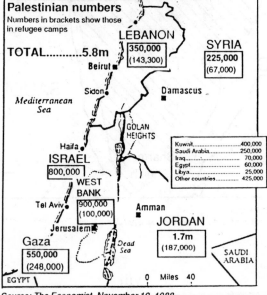

WHERE THE PALESTINIANS ARE

Palestinian numbers
Numbers in brackets show those in refugee camps

TOTAL............5.8m

Mediterranean Sea

LEBANON
350,000
(143,300)

Beirut

Sidon

SYRIA
225,000
(67,000)

Damascus

GOLAN HEIGHTS

Haifa

ISRAEL
800,000

WEST BANK
900,000
(100,000)

Tel Aviv

Jerusalem

Kuwait	400,000
Saudi Arabia	250,000
Iraq	70,000
Egypt	60,000
Libya	25,000
Other countries	425,000

Amman

JORDAN
1.7m
(187,000)

Dead Sea

SAUDI ARABIA

Gaza
550,000
(248,000)

EGYPT

0 Miles 40

Source: The Economist, November 19, 1988

ix

CHRONOLOGY OF EVENTS

Ken Tancock

1516-1918	-- Ottoman Empire (Turkey) controls most of the Middle East, with Palestine part of the province of Syria.
1881	-- Czarist pogroms in Russia spark the first modern Jewish migration and settlement in Palestine, supported by Baron de Rothschild.
1896	-- Theodore Hertzl publishes <u>Der Judenstaat</u> (The Jewish State).
1897	-- First World Zionist Congress meets at Basle, Switzerland under the leadership of Hertzl.
1900-1914	-- Zionist immigration and settlement begins in Palestine with aim of creating an exclusive Jewish society alongside that of the Palestinians.
1914-1918	-- World War I: Turkey (the Ottoman Empire) is defeated by the British, French and Arabs, the Arabs having been promised national independence by the British.
1916	-- Sykes-Picot agreement provides for France to control Lebanon and Syria and Britain to control Palestine and Iraq.
1917, Nov. 2	-- Balfour Declaration: Lord Balfour of Great Britain promises, in a letter to Baron de Rothschild, a national home for the Jewish people in Palestine on condition that "nothing shall be done to prejudice the civil and religious rights of existing non-Jewish communities in Palestine, or the rights and political status enjoyed by Jews in any other country."
1918	-- End of the War. Britain gets control of Palestine, France of Lebanon and Syria.
1919, June 28	-- Treaty of Versailles and Covenant of League of Nations signed. League Covenant contains Article 22 which established the mandate system.
1919, Aug. 28	-- King-Crane Commission reports to the Peace Conference recommending that the Zionist program to establish a Jewish state in Palestine be abandoned, as it would trespass too gravely upon the rights of the Palestinian people.

1

1920, July 1	-- Britain establishes civil administration in Palestine; Herbert Samuel, High Commissioner.
1920, Easter Sunday	-- Arab protests and rioting against Jewish immigration.
1921, May	-- Second violent Arab protest against Jewish immigration.
1923, Sept. 29	-- Council of League of Nations confirms a mandate for Palestine submitted by Great Britain; terms drawn up by British government and Zionists but Arabs neither consulted nor participants; rejected by Arabs.
1923, Oct.	-- First census taken.
1929, Aug.	-- Arab riots break out in protest against the Mandate and Jewish immigration.
	-- Britain issues the Passfield Memorandum stressing equality of Zionist and Arab claims; rejected by Arabs.
1933	-- Hitler and Nazis come to power in Germany; begin persecution of German Jews.
1936-1939	-- Arab rebellion occurs.
1939, May 17	-- Following the London Round Table Conference, Britain issues the MacDonald White Paper limiting Jewish immigration, inter alia.
	-- Zionists call general strike and use violence against British and Arabs.
1939, Sept.	-- World War II breaks out; Arabs and Jews of Palestine put aside opposition to British policies and support Britain.
1939-1945	-- World War II: Nazis carry out Final Solution to the "Jewish Problem," killing millions of Jews in the Holocaust.
	-- Jewish immigration to Palestine continues illegally and many immigrants are interned on Cyprus by British.
1940, Nov. 25	-- the ship Patria, loaded with 252 illegal Jewish immigrants, is sunk in Haifa harbour.
By 1940 there were three Jewish armed groups in Palestine: The Jewish Agency's Haganah, including an elite striking force, Palmach; and two terrorist groups: Irgun Zvai Leumi and its more radical, anti-British branch, the Stern Gang.	
1942, May	-- Biltmore Program: new demands for a Jewish state drawn up by Zionists meeting at the Biltmore Hotel in New York.

1944, Nov. 6	-- Secretary of State, Lord Moyne, assassinated by Stern Gang in Cairo.
1945, May 22	-- demands of the Biltmore Program presented to the British government.
1946, July 22	-- King David Hotel blown up by Irgun Zvai Leumi under Menachem Begin. 100 government officials (British, Arabs and Jews) are killed.
1946, July 24	-- Mandatory Government issues a Statement of Information relating to acts of violence, showing collusion of Haganah, Palmach, Irgun Zvai Leumi and Stern Gang in a program of terrorism co-ordinated by the Jewish Agency.
1947, April 2	-- Great Britain, unable to find a solution to the problems in Palestine, requests that the question of Palestine be placed on agenda of next meeting of General Assembly of United Nations.
1947, May 13	-- UNSCOP - United Nations Special Committee on Palestine created by General Assembly; Arab Higher Committee refuses to recognize its legitimacy.
1947, Nov. 29	-- General Assembly Resolution #181 (II) adopts plan for dividing Palestine; recommends creation of a Jewish state, an Arab state and an international zone for Jerusalem and environs; British to withdraw on 15 May, 1948; the two states to be created two months later.
1948, March 19	-- Violence causes U.S. to recommend to Security Council that a temporary trusteeship be established for Palestine; not accepted.
1948, April 9	-- Massacre of Deir Yassin: over 250 men, women and children killed by Irgun under Menachem Begin, with cooperation of Stern Gang; sets pattern for Zionist terror campaign to drive Arabs from new State of Israel before it officially exists.
1948, May 11	-- Lydda "death march".
1948, May 14	-- Zionists proclaim new State of Israel two months early; seize more territory than was assigned to them, 77% of Palestine instead of 56%; greater part of Jerusalem seized by Zionists; three-quarters of a million men, women and children (Muslims and Christians) dispossessed and forcibly expelled.

1948, May 15	-- British forces leave; Arab armies enter Palestine; Trans-Jordan moves to occupy the part of Palestine awarded to the Palestinian Arabs.
1948, July 15	-- Security Council orders a cease-fire.
1949, May 11	-- Israel admitted as a member of the UN on condition of readmitting Arab refugees.
1949, Dec. 11	-- UN Resolution #198 (III) on Refugees, providing for the exercise of their right to make a free choice between return to their homes or compensation.
1949	-- Israel transfers parliament and government from Tel Aviv to Jerusalem and declares Jerusalem its capital in defiance of the UN.
1955, Feb. 28	-- Major Israeli raid on Gaza; 38 Egyptian soldiers killed.
1956, Oct. 29	-- The Kafr Qasem 'massacre' on the eve of Israel's attack on Egypt in which 47 Palestinians lost their lives.
1956, Oct. 29	-- War breaks out as Israel, Britain and France attack Egypt over Egypt's nationalization of the Suez Canal; Security Council (including both U.S. and USSR) order Britain and France out and Israel to withdraw from Gaza and Sinai; UN peace-keeping force created, with a Canadian, Lester B. Pearson, playing a crucial role.
1957, June 4	-- Arab League announces a boycott of all firms selling goods and services to Israel until Israel rights the wrongs it has committed against the Palestinian people.
1964, May 28	-- PLO (Palestine Liberation Organization) created by Arab League as representative and spokesman of the Palestinians; becomes member of League of Arab States.
1967, May 18	-- President Nasser of Egypt requests withdrawal of UNEF (UN peace-keeping force).
1967, May 22	-- Nasser closes Gulf of Aqaba to Israeli shipping.
1967, June 5	-- Six Day War begins; Israel occupies West Bank, Gaza Strip, Golan Heights, all of Jerusalem.
1967, June 8	-- Israeli planes bomb USS Liberty, killing 34 American seaman and wounding 164.
1967, Nov. 22	-- Security Council Resolution 242 demands, inter alia, Israeli withdrawal from occupied territories.
1970, Sept. 6	-- 4 airliners hijacked by PFLP (Popular Front for the Liberation of Palestine; leader George Habash).
1970, Sept. 17	-- PLO expelled from Jordan; new bases formed in Lebanon.

1972, May 8	-- Sabena airliner hijacked at Lod airport; stormed by Israelis.
1972, May 30	-- PFLP calls in three Japanese "Red Army" men who shoot up Lod airport, killing 25, wounding 78 ("revenge for Deir Yassin," said PFLP).
1972, Sept. 5	-- Munich Olympics; 11 Israeli athletes and 4 Arabs killed in shootout. Israeli response: invasion of Lebanon, air strikes on Palestinian camps, killing 300-500 Palestinians, mainly women and children; Syrian villages attacked. This pattern continues intermittently throughout the '70's and '80's: attack by Palestinians, massive retaliation by Israelis (often bombing of civilians unconnected with the "terrorist" attack); houses of relatives of the suspected "terrorist" often destroyed.
1973, Oct. 6	-- Outbreak of Yom Kippur War.
1973, Dec. 21	-- Geneva Conference convenes; Israel, Egypt, Jordan, U.S., USSR represented.
1974, Oct. 29	-- Arab League Conference at Rabat, Morocco, passes resolution recognizing the Palestine Liberation Organization as "the sole legitimate representative of the Palestinian people".
1974, Nov. 13	-- Yasser Arafat, head of PLO, addresses UN General Assembly; PLO given observer status in UN.
1975, April 14	-- Sectarian civil war erupts in Lebanon.
1975, Nov. 10	-- UN General Assembly declares Zionism to be a form of racism.
1976, May 31	-- Syrian army enters Lebanon to assist Christian forces; later on attacks Tel al-Zataar Refugee Camp.
1977, Nov. 19	-- President Sadat of Egypt visits Jerusalem.
1978, March	-- Litani operation; Israel attacks Lebanon to remove PLO "terrorists".
1978, Sept. 17	-- Camp David Peace Accords signed by Egypt, Israel and U.S.
1979, March 26	-- Peace Treaty signed between Israel and Egypt; rejected by all other Arab states.
1981, June 6	-- Israel bombs and destroys Osirak nuclear reactor near Baghdad, Iraq; Israel by this time has her own nuclear weapons.
1981-1982	-- Tacit agreement between Israel and the PLO in Lebanon gives a year free of attacks on Galilee Border.

1982, June 4	-- Israeli ambassador Argov critically wounded in London; Israel accuses PLO and uses incident as an excuse to launch "Peace-for-Galilee" invasion of Lebanon.
1982, Aug.-Sept.	-- Ariel Sharon sends huge Israeli army north of Litani River as far as Beirut in order to finally destroy PLO.
	-- Beirut besieged and bombed; PLO fighters are evacuated from Beirut with promise to Arafat that U.S. would protect Palestinian civilians in Beirut refugee camps of Sabra and Shatila.
	-- Lebanese Falangists (Maronite Christians) enabled by Israeli Defence Forces to enter undefended camps and massacre about 900 civilians after the fighting has stopped.
	-- For first time anti-war opposition arises in Israel.
1985	-- Israel withdraws from Lebanon leaving a Lebanese army in South Lebanon, a force actually controlled by Israel; 30,000 Lebanese and Palestinians died as a result of the Israeli invasion.
1986-1987	-- Efforts proceed to convene a UN-sponsored conference on peace in the Middle East but Israel refuses to recognize PLO; U.S. supports Israel's position.
1987, Dec. 9	-- Beginning of the <u>Intifada</u> (Palestinian uprising) in the West Bank and the Gaza Strip.
1988, July 31	-- King Hussein abandons all Jordanian claims to the West Bank and dissolves Jordan's lower house of parliament, which included representatives of West Bank Palestinians.
1988, Nov. 15	-- Palestine National Council meeting in Algiers proclaims the establishment of an independent Palestinian State, based on UN Resolution 181 partitioning Palestine, thereby accepting a two-state solution.
1988, Dec. 14	-- the United States agrees to initiate direct talks with the PLO on "substantive issues".
1988, Dec. 15	-- UN General Assembly votes for an international peace conference on the question of Palestine, supported for the first time by all members, except for negative votes by Israel and the U.S., and abstentions by Canada and Costa Rica.

-- UN General Assembly votes to seat the State of Palestine as an observer and to substitute a UN interim force to supervise the withdrawal of Israeli occupation forces.

PALESTINE AND THE PALESTINIANS: HISTORICAL OVERVIEW

Lorne M. Kenny

I. Origins

The conflict in Palestine is the struggle of two peoples, the Palestinians and the Jews, over the same small piece of land, an area not more than half the size of the province of Nova Scotia. The Jews were seeking a haven from the persecution and discrimination they had suffered for centuries, mainly in Europe. Their goal was a state of their own in Palestine, a land occupied and ruled by their forefathers between two and three thousand years earlier. The central problem in the implementation of this goal arose from the fact that Palestine was already occupied by a people, the Palestinians, who had now lived there for well over a millenium.

First of all, let us look at the history of this area and the development of the idea of Zionism.

The Judaic, Christian and Islamic Epochs

Both the Arabs and the Israelis trace their origins back to the Patriarch Abraham. The Hebrew tribes, known as the Children of Israel, embarked on the conquest of Canaan (as Palestine was then known), in the 13th-12th centuries B.C. at about the same time as the Philistines (from which the name 'Palestine' derives) were taking possession of the coastal area. The Israelite kingdom reached its apex under King David about 1000 B.C. While it split in two about 933 B.C., the Northern Kingdom lasted until 722 B.C. and the Kingdom of Judah until the Babylonian exile in 586 B.C. After some centuries of subjection to other powers, an attempt to restore an independent kingdom ended with the Roman conquest of the area in 63 B.C. Upon the outbreak of a major revolt in 66 A.D., the Romans undertook the reconquest of the country, taking Jerusalem by storm in 70 A.D. and destroying the Temple. After further revolts, the Emperor Hadrian finally expelled all Jews from Jerusalem in 135 A.D.

Palestine was also the birthplace of Christianity, which became the dominant religion of the Eastern Mediterranean lands. The Christian community was, of course, composed of converts from among the Jews and other peoples native to the region, including certain Arab tribes, most notably the Ghassanids. The Arab Muslim conquest of Palestine was completed in 640 A.D., but it took a further century or more for the majority of the population to embrace the Muslim faith. It should be remembered, however, that some 10-15 percent of the Palestinians still adhere to the Christian faith.

The first four Muslim caliphs (i.e. 'successors' to the Prophet Muhammad) ruled from Arabia, after which Damascus became the seat of an Arab Empire for nearly ninety years. Except for the interlude when a series of small Crusader kingdoms ruled parts of the Eastern Mediterranean basin in the twelfth and thirteenth centuries, the region remained under a succession of Muslim regimes down to the end of World War I. The Ottoman Turks, because of their domination of the area for the last four centuries of this period, left an indelible impression, especially in the legal field, with many of their land tenure regulations still in force down to the present. It should be pointed out that the Turks never constituted more than a small elite majority and that the Arabs of Palestine and the rest of Syria continued to maintain their own language and culture.

From this brief survey of some 3100 years of history down to World War I, it seems clear that the Jewish people were the major occupiers of Palestine and the Jordan Valley for the first 1300 years; that from the latter part of the first century to the end of the seventh, the Aramaic and Greek-speaking Christians formed the major part of the inhabitants; and that the present-day Arabs of Palestine are the descendants of all the peoples who had lived in the area -- Jews, Philistines, Phonecians and local Arabs, as well as Arab tribesmen from Arabia.

The modern Zionists claim exclusive rights to Palestine on the basis of God's promises to Abraham and his descendants, as recorded in the Old Testament Scriptures, and on their occupation of a large part of the country, which continued, though with interruptions, for some 1300 years, after which the Jews remained a small minority of the population until the present century. The rights of the Palestinians to their homeland, however, rest on the basis of their presence there for the last thirteen hundred years and on the dominance of their language and culture in the area throughout this period, except in the Israeli enclave for the past forty years. Their title to the land is supported by the "statute of limitations", a widely accepted principle of international law whereby ancient rights, if fallen into disuse, are superseded by other rights established by a long period of usage.[1]

The Birth of Political Zionism

Zionism may be defined as a movement to achieve the social, economic and cultural rebirth of the Jewish people on their own land and in their own state in Palestine. There had always been a small Jewish minority living in Palestine and the hope of returning to the holy city of Jerusalem never died out among the diaspora. It was not until the pogroms following the assassination of Czar Alexander II of Russia in 1881 that political Zionism was born and the organized emigration of Jews from Europe to Palestine began. Most Jews in Western Europe were assimilationist in outlook at this time, but the presence of anti-semitism there convinced many of them that they must have a homeland of their own. One such was Theodore Herzl who, disillusioned by the Dreyfus case[2] which he was covering in Paris for a Vienna newspaper, wrote a slim volume entitled Der Judenstaat (The Jewish State). This book, published in 1896, became a landmark in the history of Zionism and was followed in 1897 by the first Zionist Congress in Basle, Switzerland. Various locales for the proposed Jewish state were considered and it was not until 1905 that the final decision to focus all their efforts on Palestine was taken. By 1900, twenty Jewish agricultural settlements, supported by the rich Jewish banker, Edmond de Rothschild, had been founded in Palestine, with a renewed spurt of immigration occurring on the heels of another series of pogroms in Russia after the turn of the century. Nevertheless, it is estimated that the total number of Jews in Palestine at the end of World War I in 1918 did not exceed 56,000 -- less than 10 percent of the total population.

The starting point of the dispossesion of the Palestinians from their homeland was the Balfour Declaration issued by the Foreign Minister of the British Government on November 2, 1917, promising "a national home for the Jewish people" in Palestine, though explicitly stipulating that "nothing shall be done which may prejudice the civil and religious

---

[1] See the article by the famous British historian, Arnold Toynbee, "Jewish Rights in Palestine," The Jewish Quarterly Review, N.S., vol. 52 (1961-62), p. 8.

[2] Dreyfus, a Jewish officer in the French Army, was framed as a traitor and condemned to penal servitude in 1894.

rights of the existing non-Jewish communities"[1]. The deliberate omission of the mention of the Arab population by name, or their political rights, should be noted. The incredible ignorance of Western leaders at the 1919 Versailles Peace Conference was compounded by an utter disregard for the rights of the supposedly nomadic and uncivilized inhabitants. As for consulting their wishes in the matter, Lord Balfour declared in a memorandum to Lord Curzon on 11 August, 1919 -- "So far as Palestine is concerned, the Powers have made no statement of fact which is not admittedly wrong, and no declaration of policy which, at least in the letter, they have not always intended to violate."[2] By the end of World War I the Arab population was bitterly opposed to Zionist plans, as illustrated by the fact that 72 percent of the petitions received by the King-Crane Commission appointed by the United States Government in 1919 were concerned with the threat of Jewish immigration.

The ambitions of the Zionists are revealed by the proposal their leader, Chaim Weizmann, made at the Peace Conference that the northern border of the Jewish homeland should be set at the Litani River, which flows into the Mediterranean between Tyre and Sidon in Lebanon. Is it any wonder, then, that the Jerusalem Post of June 19, 1946, should term what Weizmann had just said about "stretching out his hands to the Arabs in friendship" as so much "pretence"? Golda Meyerson (later 'Meir') had warned the Arabs at the May Day rally of that year that "nothing would swerve the Jews from their goal."

The rise of political Zionism, then, has been a recent historical phenomenon, resulting from events in Europe. It is obvious that neither the Arabs in general nor the Palestinians in particular had anything to do with the events which led to the emigration of Jews from Europe, either in the earlier period or during the Nazi persecution of the Jews, culminating in the Holocaust of World War II.

II. The British Mandate Period

The Initial Period, 1922-1928

Britain's interests in Palestine stemmed from her imperial interests in the Middle East, as evidenced in the 1916 Sykes-Picot Agreement between Britain and France to divide up control over the area between

---

[1] See Doreen Ingrams, <u>Palestine Papers, 1917-1922: Seeds of Conflict</u>, p. 18.

[2] Ingrams, p. 73.

them. Great Britain was also anxious to preserve freedom of navigation through the Suez Canal, that "lifeline" between Britain and her Empire in the Far East. Thus she was determined to maintain control over Palestine or at least to insure the existence of a friendly state there. The mandate system, devised by the newly formed League of Nations in 1919, allocated the Mandate of Palestine to Great Britain in 1922. Although the mandate powers were given the responsibility of guiding the mandated territories toward independence, the British Government was also authorized to implement the Balfour Declaration in Palestine. The Zionist dream, however, could not be realized without a bitter and ongoing struggle between the indigenous Palestinians and the Zionist Jews, the vast majority of whom were recent immigrants from Europe. The outcome has been the displacement of the larger part of the Palestinian people and the subjugation of the rest to Israeli rule. Communal violence broke out as early as Easter, 1920 and again in 1921 and 1922.

The resistance of the Palestinians was weakened by the horizontal and vertical cleavages in their society and the split in their leadership between the two real clans: the Nashashibis and the Husaynis. Sir Herbert Samuel, High Commissioner (1920-25), had sought to placate the more militant Huseynis by appointing one of their most active younger members, al-Haji Amin, as Mufti of Jerusalem and head of the Supreme Muslim Council.

As evidence that the British did make some effort to balance the interests of the two communities, it is pointed out that Sir Herbert Samuel was violently criticized by the Zionists for recommending a limitation on Jewish immigration and the development of the country "to the advantage of all of its inhabitants." A new definition of British policy was given in Winston Churchill's "White Paper" of 1922, the first official document to mention the predominantly Arab population by name, also denying any intention of subordinating them or their language or culture in Palestine. The White Paper proposed to set up a Legislative Council composed of ten appointed members, ten elected Arab members and two elected Jewish members. The Arabs, then 89 percent of the population, rejected the proposal on the grounds that their representatives could be outvoted by the other twelve.

From 1922 to 1928, the country remained sullenly, though superficially quiet. In the latter year, the World Zionist Organization was transformed into the Jewish Agency for Palestine, organized as a state through its subsidiaries:

a. The Jewish National Fund for the acquisition, for the Jewish immigrants, of land which, once obtained, was never to be alienated from the Jewish people.
b. The Histadrut, a powerful federation of labour unions, in general exclusively Jewish, which also served as capitalist entrepreneur, banker, insurance company and landowner.
c. The Haganah, or Jewish militia.

The Escalation of Violence, 1929-1939

It is not strange, then, that violence broke out again in 1929, upon which another White Paper was issued, promising to control the sale of land to the Jews, though this was never put into effect. It may be noted here that much of the land bought by the Jews was sold to them by absentee landlords, particularly in Beirut. In 1933 the Nazi Hitler regime came to power in Germany and its persecution of the Jews resulted in the increase of Jewish immigration into Palestine from an average of 9,000 per year until 1932, to 30,000 in 1933 and 62,000 in 1935, resulting in the swelling of the Jewish population from 86,000 in 1922 to 400,000 in 1936. Acts of violence by the Arabs against the Mandate Government escalated into a full-scale revolt lasting from 1936-1939.

Upon the outbreak of the Revolt in 1936, the Peel Commission was appointed to investigate its causes, but its recommendation in 1937 for the partition of the country was rejected by the Arabs. After the failure of the London Round Table Conference in 1939, the British finally issued a White Paper on the eve of the outbreak of World War II, proposing the limitation of Jewish immigration to 15,000 per year for five years and the High Commissioner's control of land transfers to Jews. The Zionist furor at what they regarded as a "breach of faith" found expression in terrorist activities against both Arabs and the British administration, and in the illegal smuggling of Jews from Europe into the country.

The World War II Period, 1939-1945

The 1939 White Paper proved to be a "pyrrhic victory" for the Palestinians.[1] Exhausted by the 1936-39 rebellion, their leadership divided and with political activity repressed during the War, they proved to be no match for the growing strength of the highly organized Zionists.

---

[1] Ann Lesch, "The Palestinian Arab Nationalist Movement under the Mandate," in The Politics of Palestinian Nationalism, by W.B. Quandt, et al., p. 41.

During the War, the Jewish Agency leaders decided it would be to their advantage to cooperate in the Allied War effort, receiving, as they expected, military training and arms from the British in return. The "Stern Gang", of which Yitzhak Shamir, the present Prime Minister of Israel, was a member, however, considered the British to be their prime foe and "offered to cooperate with the Nazis on the formation of a Jewish state."[1] The Zionists pursued their goal of a national state with single-minded zeal. At a meeting in May, 1942, in the Biltmore Hotel in New York, 600 Jewish delegates from Palestine, Europe and America passed resolutions which became known as the "Biltmore Program", demanding a Jewish commonwealth with its own army under its own flag and unlimited immigration. The Jewish community in Palestine continued to grow during the War years, largely by illegal immigration from Europe, and to prepare for the inevitable showdown with the Arab majority.

The Return to Terrorism

The Stern Gang did not wait for the end of the War to strike at the British. In November, 1944, they were responsible for the assassination in Cairo of Lord Moyne, the British Minister of State for the Middle East. Together with their parent body, the Irgun, they boasted of having killed 373 people by the end of 1946, most of them civilians[2]. It was the Irgun, under the leadership of Menachem Begin, Prime Minister of Israel from 1977-1985, which blew up the British military headquarters in the King David Hotel in Jerusalem on July 22, 1946, with the loss of nearly one hundred lives. The Arabs retaliated with terrorism of their own in March, 1947 and a year later turned to military action, but too late to stem the tide of events.

The Partition Plan, November 29, 1947

The British, for their part, had suffered a tremendous drain on their resources and grown war-weary. At this time president Harry Truman of the United States, who had succeeded President Roosevelt after his sudden death in April, 1945, was urging the British to accept 100,000 Jewish refugees into Palestine at once. This proposal was incorporated into an Anglo-American Committee report in April, 1946. No agreement

---

[1] Michael Palumbo, The Palestinian Catastrophe, p. 27.

[2] R. Allen, Imperialism and Nationalism in the Fertile Crescent, p. 381.

could be reached, however, on this or further proposals put forward later in the year and at the beginning of 1947. Finally on February 18, 1947, Britain announced that she was giving up the Palestine Mandate and referring the problem to the United Nations.

A United Nations Special Committee on Palestine (UNSCOP) was appointed and, after visiting the area, in September recommended partition of the country. This Partition Plan provided for the creation of a Jewish state comprising some 56 percent of the total area, including the most fertile parts, though the Jews made up only one-third of the population and owned only 6 percent of the land, while the Arabs were left with 43 percent, with the remaining 1 percent centred on Jerusalem to constitute an international enclave. Lester B. Pearson, Canadian Under-Secretary for External Affairs at the time, played an important mediating role in ironing out contentious issues among the Powers and has therefore been dubbed by Canadian Zionists as the 'Balfour of Canada'. With the support of the United States and strong pressure on its allies and protégés, the Partition Resolution received, on November 29, 1947, the required two-thirds majority vote in the UN General Assembly. This decision is described by the historian, William Yale, in these terms: "The fact that a majority of the UN Assembly at Lake Success voted that the will of a majority of the people in Palestine should be disregarded was considered a triumph in the application to world affairs of the nineteenth-century political ideal of majority rule."[1]

The Jewish Agency accepted the Partition Plan in principle, recognizing, as it did, Jewish rights to a homeland in Palestine. This acceptance was to be a further step toward the "full redemption" of the land, providing "the most powerful lever for the grand conquest of all of Palestine," as David Ben Gurion, the first Prime Minister of Israel, had remarked about the Peel Commission plan.[2] The Palestinian majority rejected partition and demanded that the matter be referred to the International Court of Justice, but all their efforts to prevent the loss of their homeland were of no avail.

Plan Dalet and the Displacement of the Palestinians

[See Section III, "The Birth of the State of Israel".]

---

[1] The Near East, new ed., pp. 405f.

[2] Simha Flapan, The Birth of Israel: Myths and Realities, pp. 21-22.

The Proclamation of the State of Israel

In March 1948, the Zionist leaders instituted their plan aimed at seizing the whole of Palestine. On the thirtieth of that month the Jewish Agency decided to establish a provisional government in Tel Aviv, with its own flag, stamps and taxation services. As the Zero hour approached for Great Britain to relinquish their Mandate, the United Nations went through the motions of establishing a caretaker commission, but the Zionists would have none of it.

At 4:00 p.m. on Friday, May 14, 1948, Ben Gurion proclaimed the creation of the state of Israel, restoring the sovereignty lost some 2000 years before.

III. The Birth of the State of Israel

"No Room for Both Peoples"

Most of the Zionist leaders, although not all, saw the inevitability of the displacement of the Palestinians, though they may have hoped that this could be accomplished peacefully. Herzl, the author of Der Judenstaat, suggested in his diary that the Arabs of Palestine could be "spirited" across the borders by "denying (them) any employment in our country."[1] Vladimir Jabotinsky saw as early as 1925 that a Jewish majority would not be achieved except through the exercise of the "'iron will' of a Jewish armed force against the will of the country's Arab majority."[2] It was Jabotinsky's 'Revisionist' party that gave rise to the terrorist Irgun, headed by Menachem Begin, and its offshoot, the Stern Gang, of which Yitzhak Shamir was a leader. Both men became Prime Ministers of Israel.

Since the aim of the Jewish Agency leaders was to create a Jewish state in the whole of Palestine, it was only natural that they should accept the Partition Plan as a pragmatic, but only first step in this direction. The more moderate Weizmann, for years President of the World Zionist Organization, suggested that this interim period might last 20-25 years, but Ben Gurion, later first Prime Minister of Israel, was more forthright in advocating the use of force: "I do not see partition as the final solution to the Palestine question," he declared, so "after the formation of a large

---

[1] Palumbo, The Palestine Catastrophe, p. 7.

[2] Palumbo, p. 12.

army in the wake of the establishment of the state, we will abolish partition and expand to the whole of Palestine."[1] It was, therefore, logical that he should refuse to set boundaries for the State of Israel in the Declaration of Independence[2]; nor has any Israeli government subsequently done so.

What future, then, was there for the Arabs in Palestine? "There is no room for both peoples together in this country," declared Joseph Weitz, administrator in charge of Jewish colonization, in his diary in 1940; "there is no other way than to transfer the Arabs from here to the neighbouring countries, to transfer all of them ...."[3] Ben Gurion did make an attempt to persuade some Palestinian leaders that they should accept a Jewish majority in Palestine. When they rejected such a solution, he declared, "We must expel the Arabs and take their places." The idea of a 'population transfer' was used as a euphemism for the expulsion of the Palestinians from their homeland in order to make way for an influx of Jewish immigrants. Although what became known as the "transfer committee" was not appointed until October 1948, the expulsions had been going on since early 1948, well before the creation of the State of Israel! "I am for compulsory transfer," asserted Ben Gurion, "I don't see anything immoral in it."[4]

Plan Dalet (Plan D) and the Displacement of the Arabs

In order to accomplish this 'population transfer' and prevent the rise of a Palestinian state, a military plan of action, known as Plan Dalet, for the conquest of the whole of Palestine was drawn up, providing also for the "expulsion over the border of the local Arab population in the event of opposition."[5] Yigal Yadin, the Israeli Chief of Staff in the 1948 War, tells us that he drew up the nucleus of the Plan in 1944 and completed it in the summer of 1947.[6] Of the thirteen operations outlined, eight were carried out before May 15th, when the Arab armies entered those areas assigned by the United Nations to the Palestinian State. (In the main, they did not invade the section allotted to the Jews.)

---

[1] Flapan, The Birth of Israel, p. 22.

[2] Flapan, p. 34.

[3] David Hirst, The Gun and the Olive Branch, p. 130.

[4] Flapan, p. 103; Palumbo, p. 17f.

[5] Flapan, p. 42.

[6] Palumbo, p. 39.

Because of the measure of success of the Palestinian guerilla forces in the first three months of 1948, the Haganah remained essentially on the defensive, though some 30,000 Palestinians fled their homes in the face of the spread of terror and bloodshed during this period. When the Israeli forces felt strong enough and it was judged that the evacuation of British troops had reached a point where they would not be able to interfere effectively, Ben Gurion gave orders for the implementation of Plan D at the end of March, 1948. Another spur to action was the apparent waning of American support for Partition in favour of a trusteeship for Palestine, in order to avoid the widening of the conflict.[1]

Deir Yassin

One of the worst instances of terrorism in this period, though by no means isolated, was the Deir Yassin massacre. This village, located in a predominantly Jewish area on the outskirts of Jerusalem, had signed a non-aggression pact with the neighbouring Jewish settlements. In the early hours of the morning of April 9, 1948, men of the Irgun and Stern terrorist groups surrounded the sleeping village and attacked without warning. The slaughter went on all day, due to sporadic resistance, until some 256 men, women and children lay in their blood. Though the Haganah did not participate in the massacre, the Jerusalem commander, David Shaltiel, had prior knowledge of the plan, but refused to take action. Deir Yassin, which became a name for infamy around the world, was used by the Israeli forces in their psychological warfare to drive out the inhabitants of other areas. Ben Gurion and the Jewish Agency must share the responsibility for the actions of the underground armies, by refusing to take any punitive measures against them.[2]

"The Haifa Tragedy"[3]

Three days after the Deir Yassin massacre, the Irgun agreed with the Haganah to subject themselves to their command and a little over a week afterwards cooperated in a joint attack on Haifa.[4] The story of the city's fall is one of reprisal and counter-reprisal, of the use of terror tactics, of reports of the presence of the dreaded Irgun and the Deir Yassin

---

[1] Palumbo, pp. 40-45.

[2] Flapan, pp. 42 and 94; Hirst, p. 118.

[3] Palumbo, Chapter IV.

[4] Hirst, p. 129.

massacre. Haifa, where the Jews composed 55 percent of the population, had been assigned to the Jewish state under the Partition Plan. Since it was British policy to favour the stronger side in each place, they informed the local Jewish leaders that they were withdrawing their forces to the port area, without telling the Arabs. During the fighting, which ended in a Jewish victory on April 22, the Arab civilian population left in a torrent, mainly toward Acre to the north, pursued by snipers' bullets. In the city behind them, there was widespread looting by the Israelis and Christian churches were desecrated.

"The Lydda Death March"[1]

Space will not allow us to follow the progress of Plan D in the Jewish conquest of Jaffa, the area southwest of Jerusalem prior to May 15th, and of the Negev, or the overrunning of the Galilee with its towns of Tiberias, Nazareth, Safed and Acre. The story of the expulsion of the inhabitants of Lydda-Ramleh will serve to underline the reluctance of the Palestinians to leave their homes and the cruelty with which they were driven out. Some weeks earlier at a meeting to discuss the problem of leaving large Arab civilian poulations to the rear of the fighting forces, Ben Gurion had answered his questioner with a forceful gesture signifying 'Drive them out.'[2] On July 11, 1948, the inhabitants of the two towns were terrorized by Moshe Dayan's armoured forces which surged through, leaving the corpses of men, women and even children strewn along the way. To spread fear, the population was threatened with a fate similar to that of the more than eighty who had been mown down inside the Dahmash Mosque in retaliation for a grenade thrown among some Israeli soldiers after the cease fire. To the accompaniment of looting and rape over the next two days, tens of thousands were ejected toward the Jordanian lines, while Israeli planes buzzed them and Israeli soldiers drove them along mercilessly.

The people fleeing were searched, stripped of all their valuables and killed if they resisted. Without food or water, many collapsed in the 100°F heat. "By the roadside pregnant women were prematurely delivering babies," none of whom survived. Palumbo estimates that "about 1000 Arab civilians died during and immediately after the expulsion from Lydda-Ramle."[3] Among those who endured this ordeal

---

[1] Palumbo, Chapter VIII.

[2] Palumbo, p. 127; Flapan, pp. 81 and 100.

[3] Pp. 131 and 137.

was a twenty-two year old medical student from the American University of Beirut, George Habash, who swore that day he would avenge the atrocities he had witnessed. He later founded the Popular Front for the Liberation of Palestine, responsible for many guerilla attacks on Israel and Israelis.

Although the Haganah may have "avoided outright massacres like Deir Yassin," nevertheless, "through destruction of property, harassment and rumormongering, (it) was no less determined to evacuate the Arab population."[1] By the end of the War they had destroyed 350 Arab villages and towns.

According to United Nations estimates, some 770,000 Palestinians in all fled in the terror and bloodshed during the first Arab-Israeli War. In addition there were large numbers of "internal refugees" within the borders of the new Israeli State whose property had been seized because they were absent at the time of the occupation of their area, even if only a few miles away. This tragedy of the dispossession of a people, Chaim Weizmann, when made the first President of the State of Israel, described as "a miraculous clearing of the land."[2]

Peace Opportunities Missed

Simha Flapan, as a former prominent Israeli politician, and on the basis of his study of primary source materials such as the Israeli and British archives and memoirs, devotes three chapters to debunking the following myths: "Arabs Rejected the Partition and Launched War" (Myth Two); "The Arab Invasion Made War Inevitable" (Myth Five); and "Israel Has Always Sought Peace, but No Arab Leader Has Responded" (Myth Seven). It is clear that the chief obstacle to peace has always been Israel's "refusal to recognize the right of the Palestinians to self-determination and statehood"[3] in a homeland in Palestine. The same author also places the blame squarely upon Ben Gurion for thwarting American and Arab efforts to reach a truce prior to May 15, 1948.[4]

Palumbo puts the onus on Israel for failure to reach peace with the Arabs in the wake of the War.[5] The main obstacle now was the return of the refugees, to which all of the Israeli hierarchy were opposed. Ben

---

[1] Flapan, p. 96.

[2] Hirst, p. 143.

[3] Flapan, p. 232; see also p. 49.

[4] Pp. 165, 181 and 186.

[5] Chapter XI, "There Could Have Been Peace."

Gurion, supported by General Dayan, even rejected any proposal for the resettlement of the Palestinians in other Arab countries, such as Husni Za'im's offer to settle 300,000 of them in Syria -- in the hope of extending Israel's borders and annexing the West Bank. For Ben Gurion, the issue was one of "conquest, not defence -- In the Bible, as well as in history, there are all kinds of definitions of the country's borders, so there is no real limit."[1]

The Repatriation of the Palestinians Rejected to Make Way for the Ingathering of the Jews

In UN General Assembly Resolution 273 (III) of May 11, 1949, Israel was declared to be a "peace-loving state" and accepted as a member of the United Nations, on condition of her fulfilling the Partition Resolution of November 29, 1947, and the resolution of December 11, 1948, setting up the Palestine Conciliation Commission and calling for the demilitarization of Jerusalem and the repatriation of the refugees. In spite of pressure from the United States, Israel refused to accept but a token number, reserving the right to settle them wherever she wished. Her concern was to make room for hundreds of thousands of Jewish immigrants, and indeed inside of three years she had succeeded in doubling her population! There was not room for both the newcomers and the Palestinian refugees: the Arabs in Palestine had owned 50 percent of the citrus groves, 90 percent of the olive groves and 10,000 shops and other businesses.[2] "It is difficult," admitted Joseph Schechtman, an expert on 'population transfer', "to overestimate the tremendous role this lot of abandoned Arab property has played in the settlement of hundreds of thousands of Jewish immigrants ...."[3]

Israel made every effort to encourage the Jews dispersed though the Arab World from Iraq to Morocco to immigrate to Israel. Regarding the claim that the Jews of Iraq were terrorized into leaving, this is true; but it was a Zionist ring which was responsible for the bombs and leaflet campaign, as established by investigations in Iraq and the publication in Israel by the perpetrators of details of their exploits.[4]

---

[1] Palumbo, p. 183; see also pp. 181ff and 190.

[2] Palumbo, p. 146.

[3] Flapan, p. 107.

[4] Hirst, pp. 155-164; Palumbo, pp. 198-200.

21

From War to War

Thus was the Zionist dream implemented in the establishment of the State of Israel. Founded in violence and bent on expansionism, it has not been able to live without violence. In October 1956, it was the prime mover, in collusion with Britain and France, in the Tripartite invasion of Egypt. Having swept across the Sinai in a lightning campaign, she was, however, forced to give it up again at the concerted insistence of the United States and Russia. When on May 22, 1967, President Nasser of Egypt closed the Gulf of Aqaba to Israeli shipping, Israel opted for a preemptive strike against Egypt, Syria and Jordan. In the ensuing Six Days War, she was able to seize the Sinai Peninsula and the Gaza Strip from Egypt, the West Bank from Jordan and the Golan Heights from Syria, loosing a new flood of refugees and extending the territory under her control, which she claims as her divine right, to four times that originally allotted to her. Egypt, unable to secure Israel's withdrawal in accordance with UN resolution 242 which denounces the acquisition of territory by force, launched an attack across the Suez Canal into the Sinai on October 6, 1973, smashing the Bar Lev Line on the east bank. Israel was able, however, with massive American emergency aid, to snatch victory out of defeat.

In September 1978, peace was hammered out between Egypt and Israel at Camp David, by which the rest of the Sinai Peninsula was returned to Eygpt and the Palestinians promised a kind of 'autonomy' ("for the people, not the land!" Begin afterwards explained). With her hands thus freed, and although a stable ceasefire between the P.L.O. and Israel had been in place for eleven months, Israel in 1982 invaded Lebanon, with enormous loss of civilian life, both to Palestinians and Lebanese, and tremendous material destruction. Through puppet Lebanese forces, she still controls Southern Lebanon.

We cannot avoid asking when and how the Palestinian-Israeli conflict will end. Since security cannot be achieved on the basis of force alone without the goodwill of one's neighbours, one can only conclude that, unless the Palestinians are granted self-determination in a homeland of their own on the West Bank and the Gaza Strip, in the context of a comprehensive Arab-Israeli peace settlement, there will never be peace in the region.

IV. The Post 1948 Arab-Israeli Wars

Introduction: Israeli Militarism

Israel is ever pictured by her defenders as a tiny island of democracy, enlightenment and civilization in the midst of a sea of Arabs who are portrayed as backward, barbarous and anti-democratic. Israel is presented as the righteous David, fighting for survival against the Arab Goliath.   Her early leaders claimed that they genuinely sought accommodation with the indigenous Arab population -- but subject to the Zionist aim of establishing a Jewish majority state in Palestine. When the overwhelming Palestinian majority rejected such terms, the Zionist leaders resorted to violence, intimidation and the sword.

Israeli militarism and expansionism are grounded in four basic elements of Zionist thinking:

1.   their conviction that "Eretz Israel" (the Land of Israel) stretches from the Euphrates River to the borders of Egypt, thus including much of Syria, Lebanon and the east bank of Jordan;
2.   their insistence that "Eretz Israel" is the territory of the State of Israel, that it belongs to the Jewish people and is to be inhabited by them;
3.   their constant opposition to the idea of a Palestinian people and to any expression of Palestinian nationalism;
4.   the adamant refusal of the Zionist leaders, therefore, in spite of their official acceptance of United Nations Resolution 181, of 1947, providing for the division of Palestine into Jewish and Arab states, to countenance the creation of an independent Palestinian state.

The 1948 "War of Independence"/conquest, which resulted in the dispossession of three-quarters of a million Palestinians, was not the end of the use of military force by Israel against the inhabitants of Palestine and her Arab neighbours. "A colonial society in a post-colonial age,"[1] Israel relied on violence to force the Palestinians into subjection and to seize their property. The armistices of 1948 and 1949 did not see the end of this tactic: in the summer of 1949 the inhabitants of the village of Askelon were trucked to the borders of Gaza and dumped there to make way for a new Jewish city. Deir Yassin was followed after the 1948 War by other massacres of civilians, usually termed 'reprisals': Qibya, where 66 men, women and children were slaughtered in the sleeping village by Special Unit 101, under the leadership of Ariel Sharon (Unit 101 was "a

---

[1] David Hirst, The Gun and the Olive Branch (London: Futura, 1983), p. 172.

specialized reprisal unit" composed of volunteers, which was later merged with the paratrooper corps[1]); Kafr Qasim, where 47 were massacred on the eve of the tripartite invasion of Egypt on the night of October 29, 1956; and al-Sammu[c] and two other villages in the southern Hebron area, where "a large-scale and carefully planned military action" resulted in "the loss of life and heavy damage to property ...."[2]

This official use of terror against Palestinian civilians has been justified by various Israeli leaders. Following the 1978 Israeli invasion of South Lebanon (though not generally numbered among the Arab-Israeli wars), in which "some 2000 Palestinians and Lebanese were killed and 250,000 made refugees"[3], the noted Israeli military analyst, Ze'ev Schiff, summarized the remarks made by Chief of Staff Mordechai Gur in these words: "The Army ... has never distinguished civilian from military targets ... [but] purposely attacked civilian targets even when Israeli settlements had not been struck."[4]

Force was seen to be the only way, not only for cowing and controlling the subject Arab population and for the protection of Israel against her Arab neighbours, but also as the instrument for fulfilling Zionism's still unfinished mission of expanding into the whole of "Eretz Israel". "To maintain the status quo," declared Ben Gurion after the birth of Israel, "will not do. We have to set up a dynamic state bent upon expansion."[5] This motif helped shape the events of the four Arab Israeli wars we shall examine.

Israel asserts that the wars with her Arab neighbours have been defensive wars, with the possible exception of the 1982 invasion of Lebanon, all fought to pre-empt the Arab threat to drive Israel into the sea. Since both the Arabs and the Israelis knew that Arab threats were impossible of realization, and that on various occasions the Arabs did indicate their readiness to work out a modus vivendi, such statements regarding the defensive character of Israel's wars are both "astonishing" and "untrue".[6] Rather they were fought by Israel's "Arab-fighters", of

---

[1] Ibid., pp. 180-183.

[2] Security Council Resolution 228 Concerning Military Action by Israel on the Territory of Jordan, November 25, 1966.

[3] Noam Chomsky, The Fateful Triangle (Boston: South End Press, 1983), p. 99.

[4] Ibid., p. 181.

[5] Hirst, p. 194. Here too is recorded the censure directed by Ben Gurion and Yigal Allon at each other for not grabbing more territory for Israel during the war.

[6] Chomsky, p. 99.

whom Moshe Dayan was to become "the most typical and celebrated embodiment" during Israel's first quarter century.[1]

It should not be forgotten, too, that Israel's later wars with the Arabs have provided a ready proving ground for American newly-developed weapons. Much has also been written about Israel's role as an arms manufacturer and vendor, and also as a distributor of American arms, to Iran, for instance, and earlier of American jets to Indonesia to carry out her slaughter of the Timorese.[2]

Israel's military domination of the region has been bolstered by her development of the atomic bomb, along with her determination to prevent her Arab neighbours from acquiring a like capability. The threat of the use of military intervention, for example against the Arab oil installations, is seen as Israel's "secret weapon" to bend American policy-makers to her will.[3]

In the light of what has been said, let us turn now to a brief examination of four Arab-Israeli wars.

The 1956 Tripartite Invasion of Egypt

On February 28, 1955, the Israeli army mounted a massive raid against the Egyptian garrison headquarters in the Gaza Strip, in which 38 Egyptians were killed and 31 wounded, thus marking the end of six years of comparative quiet on the Egyptian-Israeli border. The Israeli Prime Minister at that time, Moshe Sharett, had had indirect contacts with the Nasser regime of Egypt, but a new 'get-tough' policy was instituted immediately upon Ben Gurion's return to the government as Minister of Defence a week before the raid.

Nasser had refused in 1953 to be drawn into any Western-sponsored defence alliance, but did not wholeheartedly enter into Arab regional politics until the announcement of the Turkish-Iraqi pact in January, 1955 (later to be known as the Baghdad Pact). Nasser's neutralist stance between the Eastern and Western Blocs was strengthened following his attendance at the Bandung Conference of Non-aligned States in April, 1955, when he took the opportunity of exploring with Chou En-lai, China's prime minister, the possibility of securing arms from the Eastern Bloc. Other Israeli raids on Egyptian-held territory followed throughout the year, with a particularly heavy one on August 31

---

[1] Hirst, p. 172.

[2] Chomsky, p. 26.

[3] Ibid., pp. 464-469.

25

against the Egyptian police post at Khan Yunis in the Gaza Strip. With the Egyptian Army clamoring for weapons, Nasser signed the 'Czech arms deal' the following month. These events provided Ben Gurion with the opportunity he wanted: "the 'hosts of Amalik' were re-arming in Egypt,"[1] he asserted, and the arms race was on. In November, Ben Gurion assumed the prime ministership of Israel.

In the spring of 1956, negotiations for a $200,000,000 loan to Egypt from the World Bank for the building of the High Dam at Aswan were nearing completion, with Britain and the U.S. to supply another $70,000,000. In June a critical change in the office of foreign minister of Israel took place when the more cautious Moshe Sharett was replaced by Golda Meir, who fell into step with Ben Gurion's hard-line policy. Western aid towards the building of the Dam was suddenly withdrawn on July 19, provoking Nasser to retaliate a week later with the nationalization of the Suez Canal in order to provide the necessary funds to build the Dam. According to the Paratrooper's Book, the semi-official history of the Israeli Airborne Corps, Nasser had, without knowing it, "kicked off the Suez campaign."[2] Egypt's action in nationalizing the Canal, a waterway running wholly through Egyptian territory, was declared illegal by Britain and France. Israel was a natural ally in their determination to overthrow the Nasser regime, so they laid plans, as was later revealed, for an Israeli attack across the Sinai, with British and French intervention following a week later upon Israel's reaching the Suez Canal, professedly to separate the two combatants. Nasser was able, however, to salvage a political victory from military defeat when Britain and France were compelled to withdraw their forces from the Canal Zone and Israel to evacuate the Sinai Peninsula, due to pressure from President Eisenhower of the United States and the Russian threat to send in 'volunteers' and employ rockets against the invaders.

"The Six-Day War" of June, 1967

In his definitive history of the Suez War, Kenneth Love asserts that Israel, immediately upon her being forced to disgorge the territory taken in the 1956 War, began to draw up plans to regain it, plans which "required only favourable circumstances and a political decision to be put into action."[3]

---

[1] Hirst, p. 200

[2] Ibid., p. 201.

[3] Suez: The Twice-Fought War (New York: McGraw Hill, 1969), p. 677.

This 'pre-emptive strike' launched early on the morning of June 5, 1967, against Egyptian airfields, then, cannot be regarded as a 'just war' fought to save Israel from an aggressive foe bent on her destruction. In the spring of 1967 Israel was going through a severe economic crisis. General E.L.M. Burns, Commander of the United Nations Emergency Force in the Middle East, had earlier noted Israel's tendency to blame her economic difficulties on the Arab boycott and to seek some excuse to go to war in order to break the blockade. It was his view that Israel's leaders were completely confident of their army's ability to defeat any and all of the Arab countries around them.[1] This was also the view of the Israeli generals: Mordechai Hod and Ezer Weizmann, of the Israeli Airforce, Chief of Staff Chaim Bar-Lev and General Mattityahu Peled, one of the architects of the Israeli victory.[2] "I am sure," declared Peled, "that our General Staff never told the government that the Egyptian military threat represented any danger to Israel or that we were unable to crush Nasser's army which, with unheard-of foolishness, had exposed itself to the devastating might of our army."[3]

Let us return, however, to the Arab 'provocations' which are said to have occasioned this war. First of all, there was the Arab Summit meeting held in Cairo in January 1964, at which the creation of a Unified Arab High Command was approved in principal, and also the diversion of one source of the Jordan River in Syria by canal to the Yarmuk River in Jordan, in retaliation for Israel's diversion of water from the Sea of Galilee into her own water system. Neither of these Arab proposals came to fruition, however, possibly on account of the need for caution urged on the other Arab leaders by Nasser because of their lack of preparedness for a military confrontation with Israel.

Then there was the myth of the Syrian threat from the Golan Heights, including the shelling of Israeli settlements and fishing vessels on the Sea of Galilee. What should be pointed out is that immediately upon the conclusion of the armistice agreements in 1949, the Israelis began to encroach upon the demilitarized zones, especially the good agricultural land overlooked by the Golan Heights east of the Sea of Galilee and in the Lake Huleh region farther north. Fortified settlements were erected, military personnel, in the guise of police, were sent in and the work of the Mixed Armistice Commission obstructed by the Israelis. The 'curtain-raiser' for the 1967 War was the massive Israeli retaliation

---

[1] Between Arab and Israeli (London: Harrap, 1962), pp. 283, 290.

[2] Chomsky, p. 100; Hirst, pp. 210f.

[3] Hirst, p. 211.

on April 7 to the Syrian shelling of an Israeli tractor working on Arab land, in which six Syrian planes were shot down, one over Damascus. Nasser felt compelled to act in accordance with the Egyptian-Syrian Defence Pact and to answer the taunts from other Arab capitals of his lack of action. On May 16, he therefore requested the withdrawal of UNEF from Egyptian soil (Israel had never allowed UNEF to operate on its territory). Fateful consequences were to follow.

Another factor in the escalation of violence was the increasing ferocity of Israeli 'reprisal' raids on Arab territory, especially Jordanian, prior to the June 1967 War, in spite of the fact that the military threat to Israel from Jordan was minimal.

Did these Arab "provocations" merit plunging the area into war, when from January to June not one Israeli was killed as a result of Syrian shelling, and only one due to the action of Arab infiltrators? It is conceded by most observers that Nasser fell into the trap set for him by the Israelis. Although Nasser was pictured in the Western media as a swaggering warmonger, yet he had neither the means nor the intention of attacking Israel. "I do not believe that Nasser wanted war," Yitzhak Rabin, the Israeli Chief of Staff later admitted. "The two divisions he sent into Sinai on May 14 would not have been enough to unleash an offensive against Israel. He knew it and we knew it."[1] Even Menachim Begin, the former Irgun terrorist leader and later Prime Minister of Israel, while maintaining that "this was a war of self-defense in the noblest sense of the term," admitted that Nasser's action did not prove that he was about to attack. "We decided to attack him,"[2] he later admitted.

There is a good deal of evidence to support Nasser's claim that his intention was to have the UN Force withdraw only from Egypt's border with Israel in order to deter an Israeli attack on Syria. When told by U Thant, the UN Secretary-General, that it was all or nothing, Nasser then asked for the complete evacuation of UNEF and took the fateful step of blockading the strategically important Straits of Tiran at the mouth of the Gulf of Aqaba.[3] With the die already cast, King Hussein of Jordan on the 30th of May flew to Cairo to sign a joint defence agreement with Nasser. He thus exposed his forces to fiery destruction, once the Egyptian Airforce had been wiped out on the ground, giving Israel the

---

[1] Ibid.

[2] Chomsky, p. 100.

[3] Robert Stephens, Nasser, a Political Biography (London: Allen Lane, 1971), pp. 474, 478ff.

coveted prize of the West Bank, in addition to the whole of Sinai and the Gaza Strip.

With the Egyptian Airforce obliterated on the morning of 5 June, the Israeli Airforce was able in the afternoon to strike and cripple the Syrian and Jordanian Airforces. By the time Jordan had accepted the UN call for a cease-fire on the 7th, Israeli forces had taken the Old City of Jerusalem and the whole of the West Bank to the Jordan River. Egypt accepted the cease-fire on the 8th, although the Israeli forces continued to drive forward, reaching the Suez Canal the next morning. Syria asked for the cease-fire to take effect early on June 9th, but on the same morning Israel launched a determined attack on the Golan Heights, occupying the Syrian base at Quneitra the next day, which brought the Six-Day War to an end.

As a result of this war, some 200,000 Palestinians fled to Jordan from the West Bank and very few were allowed back. East Jerusalem was officially annexed on 28 June and the Golan Heights effectively so in December-January 1981-82, while "creeping annexation" was instituted in the West Bank and the Gaza Strip by the expropriation of Arab land for the creation of Israeli settlements. Hardliners such as General Moshe Dayan were not content with this expansion. "Your duty is not to stop; it is to keep your sword unsheathed .... You must not call a halt -- heaven forbid!" he told the Kibbutz Youth Federation on the Golan Heights.[1]

United Nations efforts to find a solution to the Arab-Israeli Conflict resulted in Security Council Resolution 242, adopted on November 22, 1967, calling for an end of belligerency in the region, withdrawal "from territories occupied in the recent conflict" and the recognition of "secure and recognized boundaries" for every state in the region. Ambassador Gunnar Jarring of Sweden was appointed to negotiate a settlement on the basis of this resolution. Egypt indicated a willingness to accept it, if Israel withdrew from all territories occupied during the War (though allowing for demilitarized zones) and if a just settlement for the refugee problem was found. Israel, for her part, refused any withdrawal of her forces in advance of direct negotiations with the Arab States or to specify her territorial aims. As for the Palestinian refugees, they would have to be resettled in the Arab countries, not repatriated to Israel.

When the Jarring mission ended in failure, a 'war of attrition' between Egypt and Israel ensued, with Israeli planes bombing targets throughout the Delta and even Upper Egypt almost at will. Exposed to constant bombing and bombardment, the Egyptian cities in the Canal Zone were made virtually uninhabitable, with the result that most of their

---

[1] Hirst, p. 221.

remaining inhabitants fled to Cairo and other cities in the Delta and Upper Egypt. The Rogers Plan for a cease-fire between Egypt and Israel was accepted by Nasser some two months before his death on September 28, 1970, but none of the basic issues had been settled.

The 1973 "October War" (also called the "Yom Kippur" War by the Israelis and the "Tenth of Ramadan War" by many Arabs)

The cease-fire of 1970 led merely to a "no-peace no-war" interlude which the Political and Strategic Studies Centre in Cairo concluded was to the benefit only of Israel, the United States and possibly Russia. In order to break out of this impasse and to win support from the United States, President Sadat of Egypt, in the summer of 1972, expelled the thousands of Russian 'advisers' in Egypt, but to no avail. His warning that their only recourse, then, was to take back their territory by war was not taken seriously by either Israel of the United States. Both Egypt and Syria began an arms build-up with Russian aid, though not to the extent they wanted. Early on the morning of October 6, 1973, the Egyptian forces stormed across the Suez Canal and breached the sandy levees of the Bar Lev Line with their water cannon.

There is no question about the fact that it was the Egyptians who attacked first, but it must be remembered that the Sinai Peninsula was Egyptian territory which they were trying to regain. Sadat's major aim, it would seem, was not to defeat Israel on the field of battle, for as soon as the massive American airlift of arms got underway to replace Israeli losses, he realized the futility of trying to fight the United States as well as Israel, as he said. Fierce tank battles, among the largest ever fought in the history of warfare, raged over the Sinai Desert.

On the northern front, the Syrian army, with the assistance of Jordanian and Iraqi forces and some units from Morocco and Saudi Arabia, managed to regain most of the Golan Heights, only to lose it again to the advancing Israeli forces. In response to a UN Security Council resolution, an initial cease-fire was instituted on the Egyptian front on October 22. When this broke down, fighting continued for two more days. Finally, on October 24 a more or less effective cease-fire came into effect on both the Egyptian and Syrian fronts.

A notable feature of the war was the use of the 'oil weapon' by the Arab World, with a complete embargo imposed on those considered Israel's closest friends: the United States, the Netherlands and South Africa. Prices shot up as production was cut. Some recipient countries did modify their Middle Eastern policies, but the goal of forcing Israel to evacuate the territories she had occupied in 1967, including East Jerusalem, was not reached.

Some Egyptians thought that their army should have struck across the desert toward Israel itself, but Sadat's primary aim was to involve the U.S. seriously in the peace process, and in this he succeeded in the person of Henry Kissinger, President Nixon's National Security adviser. With Kissinger's assistance, a disengagement agreement between Israel and Egypt was reached in January, 1974, whereby all Israeli forces were withdrawn from the Canal's west bank and their siege of the Egyptian Third Army in Sinai was lifted. It was not until May that a similar agreement was reached with Syria.

The initial victory of the Egyptian forces in storming the Bar Lev Line and throwing the Israeli Army back from the Suez Canal gave the Arabs a tremendous psychological boost and punctured the myth of Israeli invincibility. The rest of the Arab World was deeply upset when Sadat threw away this advantage and broke ranks to journey to Jerusalem to prepare the way for a separate peace with the Zionist enemy. As a consequence, Egypt was, on November 19, 1977, drummed out of the Arab League. With Egypt out of the fray, Israel felt free, it is argued, to further oppress the Palestinians in the Occupied Territories and to launch her invasion of Lebanon in order to deprive the Palestinian Liberation Organization of its prime base there, without fear of a military confrontation with Syria and Jordan.

The Israeli Invasion of Lebanon

After the launching of the invasion, Israel's ambassador to the United Nations maintained that Israel was acting in self-defence, in retaliation for raids and shelling by Palestinian 'terrorists' across her northern border. Thus the operation was dubbed "Peace for Galilee". Let us examine this claim.

The view of the International Commission to inquire into reported violations of International Law by Israel during its invasion of Lebanon, given in its Report entitled Israel in Lebanon, is that:

> The attempted destruction of the national existence of the Palestinians in Lebanon is, therefore, a rejection of their right to self-determination ... an incontestable legal right in international law. The continued refusal by Israel to recognize

31

this right is the basis for the tension and violence in the Middle East.[1]

This contention is born out by the consistent rejection of Palestinian national and human rights by Israel from the time of her creation as a state. In the case of the Palestinians in Lebanon, following the bloody expulsion of the PLO from Jordan in September, 1970, Israel instituted a policy of continuously raiding their camps in the southern part of the country, their last and most important refuge. After the Israeli raids on residential areas of Beirut on July 17 and 18, 1981, President Reagan sent his envoy, Philip Habib, to negotiate a cease-fire agreement between Israel and the PLO, an agreement that the PLO meticulously observed, much to Israel's chagrin. On April 21, 1982, the Israelis bombed ostensible PLO positions in Lebanon without retaliation by PLO forces. The only PLO action across the Lebanese-Israeli border prior to the attack by a Palestinian splinter group on the Israeli ambassador in London on June 4, 1982, was the firing of 100 rounds of Katyusha rockets in reprisal for Israeli air attacks on alleged PLO bases in Lebanon on May 9. The London incident was used as pretext for the Israeli Airforce to strike heavily at PLO centres in South Lebanon, with a full-scale invasion following on June 6. The invasion had, in fact, been planned by General Eitan, Chief of the Israeli Defence Staff, for July 1981 but was postponed on account of the cease-fire arranged by Philip Habib.[2]

Israel's aim in invading Lebanon, as has been indicated, was to crush the PLO, to destroy their base there and to scatter them beyond recognition as a cohesive national unit. In addition, Israel's "first objective", according to George Ball, had to do with the West Bank, claimed by the Zionists as part of "Eretz Yisrael" (The Land of Israel), its land and water resources and its policy of multiplying Jewish settlements there. The crushing of the PLO would leave the Palestinians in the Occupied Territories at the mercy of the occupier.[3] Israel's "second objective", according to Ball, was to detach Lebanon from the rest of the Arab World by supporting Maronite separatist ambitions and forcing Lebanon to sign a peace treaty with Israel that would neutralize it. General Sharon, the architect of the invasion, dreamed of working with the Phalangists to expel the Syrians from Lebanon and the Palestinians from the West Bank, resulting in Israel's becoming the dominant power

---

[1] London: Ithaca Press, 1983, 2nd printing, p. 22.

[2] Ibid., pp. 17f.

[3] George W. Ball, Error and Betrayal in Lebanon (Washington, D.C.: Foundation for Middle East Peace, 1984), pp. 33ff.

in the Middle East.[1] It should be noted that the United States accepted the Israeli claim that this was a defensive war and that her Secretary of State, General Haig, made no effort to dissuade Israel from mounting the invasion.

The war was conducted in brutal fashion, with the strafing and bombardment of refugee camps and urban centres, with little discrimination between military targets and civilian quarters, including hospitals, schools, orphanages, mosques, etc. The latest American weapons were used, including fragmentation and incendiary bombs and what the Israeli newspaper, Ha'aretz, called the "blast bomb" or "vacuum bomb", a terror weapon of immense destructive power.[2] The target was the population as a whole, the Palestinians and all who supported them. An Israeli officer, "when asked why bulldozers were knocking down houses [in the captured camps] in which women and children were living," replied, "they are all terrorists."[3] Prime Minister Begin and his government certainly shared this view.

At the beginning of the invasion, Israel had announced that their intention was to penetrate only 40 kilometers into southern Lebanon, that is up to the Litani River. As we know, they extended their objectives to include the conquest of Beirut and the hill country overlooking it, occupied by the Druze allies of Syria. The siege of West Beirut was a bloody ordeal for the city, with indiscriminate bombardment and the use of illegal weapons and tactics such as the cutting off of food, water and medical supplies.[4]

The destruction and slaughter culminated in the horrendous massacres in the Sabra and Shatila Camps, originally set up on the outskirts of Beirut by UNWRA in 1948. Israeli complicity in facilitating the carnage is all too clearly established by eyewitness accounts, not only of Palestinians who escaped with their lives, but also by scores of foreigners, including doctors, nurses, diplomats and others. It was the IDF (Israeli Defence Force) which sealed off the camps on Wednesday, September 15, 1982, letting no one in or out, which agreed with the Phalangist militia leaders to allow their men into the camps for "mopping up" and "to clear out terrorist nests," to use General Sharon's words, and

---

[1] Ball, pp. 27-29; Israel in Lebanon, pp. 6f.

[2] Chomsky, pp. 214ff.

[3] David Shipler in Chomsky, p 217.

[4] Israel in Lebanon, chpt. 14, "The Siege of Beirut," pp. 143ff.; Chomsky, pp. 224ff.

which supplied bulldozers used to bury the dead in mass graves and to level their homes.[1]

Some 20,000 Palestinian and Lebanese, most of them civilians, lost their lives in the invasion -- the highest civilian to military casualty rate in any war during this century. It is estimated that about 15,000 were taken prisoner and kept in internment camps in southern Lebanon under inhuman conditions, including beating and torture, or were transported, contrary to international law, to Israel.[2] In addition, some 500,000-800,000 were made homeless. Israel was also charged with instituting a regime of economic domination of South Lebanon.

The above brief résumé of the Israeli invasion of Lebanon makes reference only in passing to the material damage, amounting to billions of dollars, done to the Lebanese and Palestinians, for which many international jurists think Israel and its weapons supplier, the United States, should be held responsible. In addition to the catalogue of crimes by Israel in its invasion of Lebanon mentioned above, reference might be made to the fact that a majority of the International Commission of Investigation came to the conclusion that Israel had been guilty of "Genocide and Ethnocide".[3]

Conclusion

There is no doubt that Israel finds her position as a tiny island of four and a half million inhabitants in the midst of an Arab sea of nearly two hundred million people, threatening to her existence. Israel's leaders, however, continually harp upon this threat as a staple of both domestic and foreign policy, putting the blame for the unending conflict on the Palestinians and her Arab neighbours. Founded on force, Israel has opted for the continued use of force, both to subjugate the Palestinians and to enforce her will upon her Arab neighbours. She has also used war as a means of expansion from the beginning. In order to

---

[1] Chomsky, pp. 364ff.; Israel in Lebanon, chpt. 15; and F.P. Lamb (ed.), Israel's War in Lebanon: Eyewitness Chronicles of the Invasion and Occupation, 2nd ed. (Boston: South End Press, 1984), chpt. V, "Israeli Facilitation of the Sabra-Shatila Massacre." Even Israel's own Kahan Commission could not hide the facts regarding the prior knowledge and agreement of Generals Sharon, Eitan, Yaron and others -- see Chomsky, pp. 375ff., especially pp. 397-409.

[2] Chomsky, pp. 228-241; Lamb, pp. 760-762; David Gilmour, Lebanon, the Fractured Country (London: Sphere Books, 1983), p. 178.

[3] Israel in Lebanon, Appendix I, pp. 194-198.

accomplish these ends, Israel has made herself, with the support of the United States, her main weapons supplier, into the strongest and most feared regional military power. Many of her own citizens, as well as outside observers, believe that security and peace for Israel herself and her neighbours cannot be attained by force alone, but by compromise and the mutual recognition of the basic rights, human and national, of all concerned, including the Palestinians.

THE PALESTINIAN TRAGEDY: TWO PERSONAL ACCOUNTS

Sami Hadawi

I. Farewell to Home

"Mid pleasures and palaces though I may roam,
Be it ever so humble, there is no place like home."

I stood on the verandah of my home that last fateful afternoon of April 29, 1948, overlooking one of the most picturesque views of the New City of Jerusalem. The German and Greek Quarters with their white and red stone buildings, surrounded by tall pine trees, lay before me as if on a platter. In the background could be seen the official residence of the British High Commissioner perched on top of the hill and overlooking the River Jordan and the Dead Sea some 1300 feet below sea level, with the Mountains of Moab stretching across the eastern horizon. The residents of Government House -- representing the might and splendour of Great Britain -- were making ready to forsake Jerusalem.

I stood in anguish and grief for the sufferings of the City of the Prince of Peace. The hustle and bustle of a live neighbourhood were not there, the groaning of the bus as it wound its way up the hill with its load of returning residents could no longer be heard. There was the uneasy stillness of death in the air -- the stillness of an impending storm. The once attractive and lively buildings had lost their glamour; bomb-demolished homes lay crumpled to earth as evidence of man's cruelty. The atmosphere was full of awe and foreboding as to the fate of the Holy City.

Only four months before, Jerusalem had been swarming with people, while in my own home -- now a shambles -- we had celebrated Christmas, and on December 26 were on our way for a short holiday before school started again for the children. We drove up to Tiberias on our way to Lebanon and stopped for lunch on the shores of the Sea of Galilee to enjoy the famous St. Peter fish -- the fish which derived its name from the miracle by Our Lord of the five loaves and fishes -- at Capernaum immediately across the Lake from where we then sat. After lunch, we continued our journey, passing Mount Hermon to the East with its snow-covered peak shining brightly in the glowing midday sun, and started our ascent into the Lebanon Mountains. As we drove farther and farther away from Jerusalem, but only for a pleasant holiday, little did I then realize that it would be the last time that any other member of my family would see that part of Palestine or our home again.

Although partition of the Holy Land had been recommended by the United Nations less than a month before, we could not conceive that the political strife, whatever the outcome, would affect the life and position of the individual. We had hardly reached our destination when the disturbing news reached us that two buildings in the immediate vicinity of our home had been blown up as a means of frightening the population away. I decided to return alone to Jerusalem to see how I could best protect my property. On my first night in the City, I was awakened by a loud explosion which shattered some of the windowpanes of my bedroom. A family hotel, hardly two blocks away from my home, was completely demolished over the heads of its twenty-two residents. This had the desired effect of frightening the majority of the residents out of their homes, and as May 15, 1948 approached and the British administration was due to leave the country, the situation continued to deteriorate until I alone remained in the whole area that day of April 29 as I looked down on the surrounding destruction and desolation.

I gazed down into my garden -- the garden I had planned and tended with my own hands. Hundreds of Easter and Calla lilies were in full bloom, but there was no one to pick them. The children's swing was there, now empty and idle; the box of sand was deserted, while the children's picks and shovels were lying about. I recalled the pleasure I had had as I watched the children frolic and play, unaware of the treacherous days that were yet to come.

As I stood without a living soul in sight, I recalled that June day in 1931 when I had returned to Jerusalem with my bride. I remembered the hopes and plans we both had had for our future. I remembered the evening we had driven to the site of our future home; the full moon had smiled graciously upon us, throwing its silvery rays over the whole area, and suddenly there was the pealing of the church bells calling the monks to their evening prayer, lending charm and serenity to our surroundings.

I recalled, as I stood in my loneliness, how a month later my wife and I had visited the site for the laying of the foundation stone. I had carried with me a copy of the Holy Bible encased in a tin box containing, according to custom, a few silver coins for good luck. I remembered that, as I had laid the Bible under the foundation stone, I had offered a short prayer of thanks, imploring the Almighty to give us and our children protection and happiness in the home we were about to build. For "Unless the Lord build the house, they labour in vain that build it!"

I recalled the fourteen happy years we had spent in that precious home. I remembered the excitement and preparations we had made to receive our firstborn, and then our second child. I remembered the anxiety, the laughter and the joy we had experienced as we watched our children first toddle and then walk, growing from infancy into childhood, awaiting for the day when they would be on their own to visit the home where they had been born and reared, to reminisce with their own little ones over their childhood within its protective and loving walls.

As I stood there living over the past, I was suddenly awakened to reality by the sound of a bullet that hissed by, almost taking my life in its stride -- aimed by one whom I had never seen; a man to whom I had done no harm; a human being towards whom I harboured no enmity. I went inside, puzzled, desperate and heavy of heart. I moved from one room to another. All was quiet; the dust lay thick on the furniture; the windows were paneless because of the blasts as the empty homes of the residents came down one after the other. I could not restrain a shudder. I wandered from room to room as if bidding it and the furniture farewell. I stood in the dining room where only a few months before the Christmas Tree had stood. Lost in my reflection, I imagined I could see the tree brightly decorated and lighted, with our children and their cousins and friends gathered around singing "Silent Night", in celebration of the birth of the One who was like unto them. The laughter as Father Christmas distributed his presents still rang in my ears. Suddenly the piano came to life, not from the fingers of my son playing Chopin, but from the resonance of machine-gun fire.

I stood there stunned and unbelieving. I pondered over what was happening, why it should happen, and what wrong-doing I or my family or our neighbours had done to deserve to be driven away. I began to hope that it was all a dream, an ugly dream, but alas, it was real! I could not hold back a tear, and in utter despair and resignation, I moved towards the entrance. As I stood for the last time on the threshold, I took a parting look at my precious belongings and muttered a short prayer as I had done fourteen years before: "May it please thee O God that I and my family may return to this our beloved home to sing Thy praise and bless Thy Name!" I locked the door, little realizing that I was bidding my last farewell to my home.

II. The Story of Abu Hasan

The mail from Jerusalem brought me a letter from an inmate of a Palestine Arab refugee camp pleading for help for his son Mustafa, aged 15 years, to be removed from refugee camp life to a healthier environment where he could continue his education and become a useful citizen and support for his aging parents.

I had not seen Abu Hasan since January 1948, and the story he wrote was truly pathetic but hardly different from the stories of thousands of other Palestinian Arab families. His letter said:

"... We defended our beloved city of Ramle against countless Zionist attacks, but, after they received arms and ammunition from communist Czechoslovakia, the Israelis were able to break through our defenses and occupy the town in July 1948. For two days we could not leave our homes; and on the third, five Israeli soldiers broke into our home and ordered us to leave, saying: 'This is our country, and these are our homes; get out!'

"My first born, aged 16 years, tried to protect his mother and grandmother from the rough handling of the intruders, only to be shot dead. The women screamed at this cold-blooded murder. I was dumbfounded with grief. With the butts of their rifles they threw us out of our homes. We were not allowed to take anything. I was even searched and relieved of the few coins I carried on my person. We were not allowed to attend to our dead son. How and where he was buried I shall never know.

"We joined a caravan of some 40,000 who were fleeing haphazardly across open fields and up rocky mountain slopes, with machine-gun fire speeding us on our way for dear life's sake. Many fell by the wayside. My aged mother passed away from sheer exhaustion. For a grave, we could only heap stones over her dead body to protect it from wild animals and birds of prey. When we were out of immediate danger, we found ourselves in exile, exhausted, hungry and sick at heart.

"Today, after more than twelve years of this exile, we are in no better position. Our homes are tattered tents, mud huts, or caves; and we try to live on a United Nations ration which scarcely covers our minimal needs. Our children suffer from malnutrition. We have been reduced to the lowest level of humanity with no future to look forward to.

"My thoughts are not for myself, although I was well established for the future when my hopes were shattered by people to whom I owe nothing and whom I have never harmed. It is of the future of my surviving son that I now feel concerned. I want him to get away from the morbid refugee camp life to learn the meaning of human dignity and self-respect."

Abu Hasan had been a prominent member of his community in Ramle. He represented the interests of the town on Government tax assessment committees. As I read this letter, my thoughts took me back to the days before the Palestine tragedy. I remembered the picnic party he gave in my honour at his orange grove on the road between Jaffa and Ramle. Some fifty guests -- Christians, Moslems, and Jews -- had been at that party. With pride Abu Hasan had shown us around his grove, tenderly speaking of this and that tree as though they were his children.

Today, the fruit from his orange grove is shipped to Europe as an "Israeli achievement" to raise hard currency to maintain a state "not born in peace as was hoped for in the United Nations Resolution of November 29, 1947, but rather ... in violence and bloodshed," as United Nations Mediator Count Bernadotte pointed out before his assassination by the Israelis in 1948.

I could not answer the letter because Abu Hasan had failed to give his full address. I wrote to a friend in Bethlehem to try to locate him. The reply was discouraging.

"There are many Abu Hasans in refugee camps which make it impossible for me to find the man you are looking for. All of them desperately need help. They ask for human dignity, self-respect, and the return of their own property."

It seems a great pity to me, in this World Refugee Year, that dignity and self-respect continue to be denied to Abu Hasan; and his remaining son, and the children of neighbours who now huddle in miserable temporary dwellings, are prevented by blind injustice from becoming useful world citizens. Until this situation is corrected, as it must be in the name of world humanity, there can be no meaningful talk of peace and security among the nations of the world.

THE PALESTINIANS IN ISRAEL

Naji Farah, James A. Graff and Farid Ohan

By the end of the war in 1948, approximately 18 percent of the population (156,000) of the newly established State of Israel consisted of Palestinians who had refused to be intimidated into leaving their homes and land. Their numbers have continued to grow and today exceed 800,000. The Declaration of Independence had promised "complete equality of social and political rights for all citizens, without distinction of creed, race or sex". And yet, these Palestinians, citizens of the State of Israel, have yet to be granted "full and equal citizenship and due representation".

It was evident from the outset that the Zionist plan for a homeland in all of Palestine did not envisage the presence of a large non-Jewish population in their midst. The exclusivist nature of the Jewish State, coupled with exaggerated concerns about security, led the Israelis to embark upon a systematic and repressive program designed to reduce the number of Palestinians who stayed behind. The Israelis recognized that a mass expulsion of all the Palestinians, desirable as this may have been, would tarnish their image as a 'democratic' state. Instead, they chose to accomplish their objective through a series of quasi-legal and illegal maneuvers which convinced no one but their most ardent supporters in the world community. The terror tactics which had proven to be successful in inducing 750,000 Palestinians to flee their villages and towns before and during the war, were now employed to reduce the numbers of those who stayed behind.

Two months after the Declaration of Independence, Ben-Gurion called for an elimination of "Arab Islands" in Jewish population areas. On July 12, 1948, some fifty thousand Palestinians were driven out of Ramleh and Lydda, now securely within Israel's borders, the publicly stated reason being that they might cooperate with the enemy. No such evidence existed. These were Palestinians who wanted to stay in their homes and be protected by the provisions of the Declaration of Independence. Men, women, children and the elderly were forced to leave on foot from Lydda with many dying from the heat, exhaustion or enemy bullets; in Ramleh, they were bussed out by the Israeli Defence Forces. Their homes were looted and their possessions pillaged.

What was of greater consequence in the control of the Palestinians in Israel was the introduction by the government of longer term measures

41

designed to make it difficult for Palestinians to flourish and live peacefully with their Jewish countrymen. In 1948, Ben-Gurion introduced military rule to govern and regulate the lives of Palestinians living in the Jewish state. This rule derived its authority from the Mandatory Emergency Regulations (Defence Regulations) which were introduced in 1936 by the British to contain the Arab Revolt and later used against the Jewish Underground Movement. Under these rules, the army was empowered to deport or transfer individuals and whole communities; to confiscate and destroy their property and prohibit them from working; to impose curfews and imprison individuals without trial; to restrict the movement of an individual inside and outside the country and even to expel him from his native land without explanation. Palestinians, citizens of the State of Israel, to whom these regulations applied, were denied any form of legislative or judicial appeals and could only seek redress through a military court which, since accountable to no other authority, was an exercise in futility. When these very same regulations were used by the British against the Jewish Underground, one future Israeli Minister of Justice, Yaacov Shapira, said that there were no such rules even in Nazi Germany; another characterized them as 'officially licensed terrorism'.

Empowered by the Defense Regulations, the army lost no time in using them. In 1950, the inhabitants of the Palestinian village of Ashkelon were put on trucks by the Israeli Army and dumped in Gaza, then under Egyptian control. And in 1956, one of the most horrific and barbarous acts was to take place. On the eve of the Israeli invasion of Egypt, the Israeli Frontier Guard, having imposed a curfew without sufficient notice, killed in cold blood forty-seven of the villagers of Kafer Qasem, as they returned home after a long day of work in their fields. It is true that the two officers responsible for this massacre, Melinki and Dahan, were brought to trial and that they were sentenced to jail terms of seventeen and fifteen years respectively, but they were free men within a year of their sentence. Melinki, who alone killed forty-three men in one hour, was subsequently appointed 'officer responsible for Arab affairs' in the town of Ramleh.

Military administration was ostensibly introduced to contain the alleged "security threat" posed by the existence of Palestinians in the State of Israel at a time when Israel was engaged in a war with the Arabs. The fact of the matter is that these Palestinians, even if they had intended to, did not have the military means to pose such a threat. Military administration, which continued to be in effect for some seventeen years, was no more than a ploy to realize Zionist aspirations to seize and colonize the land of Palestine. It is useful to note that many of the provisions of the Defense Regulations are currently being used to accomplish the same ends in the West Bank and Gaza.

Besides the Defense Regulations, there were other measures taken that were far more Kafkaesque and Orwellian in nature. In 1950, the Law for the Acquisition of Absentee Property was passed. Ostensibly, it was designed to protect the property of Palestinian land owners made refugees in the war. What it did in practice, however, was to ensure that Palestinian property was made available for new Jewish settlements. It was the application of this Law to the Israeli Palestinians that betrayed its true intent: namely, the acquisition of more Palestinian property for Jewish immigrants. It was argued that any Palestinian who was away from his place of residence between November 29, 1947 and September 1, 1948 would be considered to be an 'absentee' without regard to the reason for his absence. But since many of these 'absentees', estimated to run into the tens of thousands, were Palestinian citizens of the newly established State of Israel, they came to be classified as "present absentees". One author describes this bizarre situation as follows: "... all his (the present-absentee's) worldly possessions -- his home and fields -- could be taken away from him and given to somebody else, a total stranger who came from across the seas. It did not matter how long he had been away; it could have been for one day only. No matter where he had gone; it could have been to the next village. No matter why he left; perhaps to buy some sheep."[1] In this manner, some five-hundred thousand acres were confiscated and given to the Development Authority which, in turn, allocated the land for the settlement of Jewish immigrants from Europe and elsewhere.

Another of these measures, used to justify the confiscation of Palestinian land by the State, was the legislation pertaining to the use of 'uncultivated land'. Under the Emergency Articles for the Exploitation of Uncultivated Areas, the Minister of Agriculture was empowered to confiscate any land which in his judgment was not being cultivated. To ensure the availability of such 'uncultivated land', the Minister of Defense would, under powers given to him by the Defense Regulations, declare some Palestinian property as a 'closed area'; that is, an area which for 'security reasons' was deemed to be off limits without special permission from the Military Governor. As Hirst puts it: "The Military Governor finds himself unable, for security reasons, to grant such permits to (Palestinian) farmers. Their fields quickly become 'uncultivated lands'.

---

[1] David Hirst, The Gun and the Olive Branch, p. 189.

43

Noting this, the Minister of Agriculture takes prompt action 'to ensure that it is cultivated'. He has done this either 'by labourers engaged by him' or by 'handing it over to another party to cultivate it'. This other party, of course, is the neighbouring Jewish colony".[1]

Today, the situation of the 800,000 Palestinian citizens of the State of Israel is somewhat improved. The measures described above, having achieved their purpose, are no longer in effect. Similar measures to achieve similar results are in use in the areas occupied by the Israelis in the 1967 war, the West Bank, Gaza and the Golan Heights. Israeli Palestinians have come to enjoy some of the original promise of equal citizenship and due process, but they remain largely a group of second-class citizens.

Though Israeli Palestinians have been granted the right to vote, they have found it difficult to exert any type of genuine influence on the Israeli political process. Any attempt on their part to organize has been thwarted by subtle pressure exerted by the authorities, especially the much feared Shin Beth (Israel's Internal Security Force). Consequently, they have had to ally themselves with fringe parties somewhat sympathetic to their plight, such as the Communist Party (Rakah). While Palestinians have run for and succeeded in getting elected to the Knesset, it is almost inconceivable that they would ever be allowed to form a Palestinian Party at the national level. First, a special committee of the Knesset must certify the eligibility of any political party to field candidates and can effectively block the emergence of an Arab party. Secondly, any attempt on their part to undertake any type of organized political action has usually been met with opposition, harassment and the use of force by the authorities. In 1976, for example, Israeli Palestinians went on a one-day strike to protest the confiscation of their lands. They were confronted by units of the Israeli army who killed six Palestinians, wounded about a hundred and detained in excess of four hundred. Although there are five Arab members of the 120-member Knesset, they are distributed among four parties, three of which compete for the Arab vote. This competition itself tends to keep a potential voting block fragmented.

But it is in conducting their daily affairs that the Israeli Palestinians have encountered the greatest discrimination and harassment. Again, while their economic lot has improved considerably since 1948, they continue to be treated as second-class citizens when it comes to the allocation of public funds. "In the 1983 budget, for example, the central government provided the Arab city of Nazareth with the equivalent of US

---

[1] Hirst, p. 190.

$629.40 per capita, compared with US $1,688 per capita in upper Nazareth, the largely Jewish town on the bluff above. The Arab village of Kfar Qara received US $231.17 per capita in public funds, while the neighbouring Jewish town of Pardes Hanna got US $1540.90 for each resident."[1] This inequitable distribution of government funds has affected all aspects of Palestinian life. In education, for example, Palestinian university students constitute no more than 3.5 percent of the total university population even though Palestinians constitute more than 16 percent of the Israeli population. In contrast, Palestinians outside direct Israeli jurisdiction have consistently attained educational levels higher than those Palestinians who have been under Israeli control since 1948. Many factors contribute to this. There are few adequate teaching facilities and properly equipped classrooms at the primary and secondary levels in Palestinian towns and villages and few properly trained and qualified teachers in the Arab sector. The teaching method in Arab schools emphasizes a traditional system of rote learning and memorization, unlike the methods used in the Jewish sector. In addition to problems Arab students face in preparing themselves for university, they face restrictive admission practices, especially to key science faculties (electronics, nuclear physics, aeronautics, etc.) for "security reasons". As a consequence, those who can go on to university are forced into the humanities and social sciences, areas in which job prospects are limited.

In their daily lives, Israeli Palestinians are subjected to harassment, usually under the pretext of 'security concerns'. Any Israeli Palestinian who wants to teach in Arab schools requires clearance by the Shin Beth. Such clearances are often predicated on the applicant's political affiliation and activity. And while Israeli Palestinians, unlike most Israelis, are not required to serve in the army and would find it almost impossible to do so if they so desired, military service has come to be the basis for rationalizing all sorts of inequitable treatment: subsidized housing loans and increased child payments. Special educational considerations are given only to those who have performed military service. There are other forms of petty harassment that go on: mail inspection, interrogation by the authorities and ethnic slurs. In general, Israeli Palestinians are made to feel unwanted and aliens in their own land.

Israel's treatment of its Palestinian citizens reflects the internal contradiction in the very nature of the state. The Zionist goal of creating an exclusivist 'state for the Jews' forces Israel to see its Palestinian

---

[1] David Shipler <u>Arab and Jew: Wounded Spirits in a Promised Land</u>, p. 445.

citizens as an obstacle to the achievement of that goal; yet its commitment to democratic ideals requires it to treat all its citizens alike, regardless of creed, race or nationality. The evidence shows that it is the Zionist ideal which has triumphed in the first forty years of the existence of the Israeli state.

THE OCCUPIED TERRITORIES

Farid Ohan

In the aftermath of the June War of 1967, Israel came to occupy that part of historic Palestine which was not taken over in 1948, namely the West Bank and the Gaza Strip. These territories had been under Jordanian and Egyptian control respectively since the 1948 War. Israel had realized the long-cherished Zionist dream of conquering all of the land of Palestine. But as was the case in 1948, this was not a "land without people for a people without a land". The occupation of the West Bank and Gaza brought under Israeli control an additional 1.3 million Palestinians, three hundred thousand of whom were expelled from their homes during and soon after the war. Many of these expelled Palestinians, refugees of the 1948 War, were made homeless for the second time in one generation.

It was clear from the beginning that in pursuing its goals, Israel was not going to be influenced by the dictates of the international community. Contrary to a unanimously adopted resolution of the Security Council of the United Nations (#242) in November of 1969, calling on Israel to withdraw its armed forces from territories occupied in the war, Israel annexed East Jerusalem soon after the war (an action which has neither been condoned nor recognized by any other country) and, twenty years later, continues to occupy the rest of the West Bank and the Gaza Strip.

Palestinians and many others claim that Israel's action throughout its forty years of existence, can be best understood in the context of the original Zionist objective for an exclusivist Jewish state in all the land of Palestine (Eretz Israel). Anything short of this objective is perceived by most Zionist leaders as a temporary setback accepted only as a result of political realities or geopolitical considerations. Consequently, this Zionist objective has been relentlessly pursued, often at the expense of moral and/or legal dictates. The conflict with the Palestinians has always been seen as a zero-sum game in which the gains of one party must be a loss to the other. Of course, while the Zionist dream has dictated the modus operandi of the Israeli state, it is never stated so publicly. Israeli violations of international law, of human rights, of United Nations resolutions are always officially explained in the name of security, of the survival of the Jewish state and the triumph of 'David over Goliath'.

Contrary to international law, as embodied in the United Nations Charter and the Fourth Geneva Convention, which specifically forbids

47

the acquisition of land through conquest, Israel has appropriated and colonized over 50 percent of the West Bank and 30 percent of Gaza. Eighty-five percent of this land, most of it farm land, belonged to Palestinians who consequently lost their only means of livelihood. The confiscation of Palestinian land has been given the garb of legality through the use of antiquated quasi-legal measures, and under the pretext of "security", a strategy which is very reminiscent of that used to acquire Palestinian land after the establishment of the State in 1948.

East Jerusalem, under Jordanian control since 1948 and with an overwhelming majority of Palestinian inhabitants, was formally annexed by Israel within a few weeks of the June War of 1967. This action, in clear violation of international law, was presented to the world as a fait accompli. The fact that the annexation of Jerusalem has not been recognized by any other country, has not deterred the Israelis from transforming East Jerusalem into an "emphatically Jewish city". Its municipal borders were extended arbitrarily and every aspect of the lives of its Palestinian inhabitants came under Israeli control and jurisdiction. The municipal council of East Jerusalem was dissolved; municipal property and records were seized; Arab banks were closed; the Israeli taxation system and Israeli currency were enforced and all professional and trade associations came under Israeli authority.

While Israel has not yet formally annexed the rest of the West Bank and the Gaza Strip, actions taken since 1967 betray a form of "creeping annexation" designed to incorporate as much of the territories as is politically feasible and expedient. The Labour Party, which was in power at the time of the war, adopted and continues to adopt what came to be known as the "Allon plan". This plan envisages a settlement in which land is exchanged for peace. Under no circumstances, however, does it consider a return to the borders which existed in 1967 (usually referred to as the 'Green Line'). East Jerusalem, with considerably extended municipal borders, and almost 40 percent of the West Bank and Gaza would be earmarked for annexation. The remaining territory, which would include areas with a high concentration of Palestinians, would be relinquished to Jordan in peace negotiations; or, in the event that negotiations do not occur, will remain under Israeli control but its inhabitants will continue to be 'stateless'. This was an ingenious plan which would allow Israel to acquire territory of its choice while at the same time preserving the Jewish nature of the state by absorbing a minimum of Palestinians.

The Labour Party was succeeded in office by the more 'hawkish' Likud Party in 1977, led by Menachem Begin. The Begin government made it clear from the beginning that, in its view, the West Bank and Gaza were part of 'Eretz Israel'. Indeed, Begin renamed the West Bank "Judea and Samaria", the Biblical names of these lands. Under the Likud government, the colonization of the conquered land was accelerated. The vanguard colonies created on the West Bank and Gaza by the pioneer zealots of the Gush Emunim (Bloc of the Faithful), were now expanded to include young Israeli families, who were attracted to form new colonies through such government measures as subsidized housing. The 'Judaization of Judea and Samaria" was in full swing. Begin's intentions were stated clearly in an interview he had with the <u>Christian Science Monitor</u>: "Gradually we have been managing to erase the physical distinction between the coastal area and Judea and Samaria. ... We haven't completely succeeded yet. But give us three or four or five years, and you'll drive out there and you wouldn't be able to find the West Bank."[1]

But Israeli plans to annex part or all of the West Bank and the Gaza Strip are made very difficult by the presence of some 1.4 million Palestinian inhabitants. The Israelis want the land but without the Palestinian people. Annexing the West Bank and Gaza with the Palestinian inhabitants would create what has come to be known as the 'demographic problem'. Given the higher birth rate among Palestinians, other things being equal, the balance of numbers will turn in their favour over the years, thus eroding the Jewish nature of the state. Gad Yaacobi, Israel's Minister for Economic Planning, projects that by the turn of the century, the non-Jewish population of Israel and the Occupied Territories will comprise 43 percent of the total population.

The occupation of the West Bank and the Gaza Strip has adversely affected the economic, political, cultural, social and educational life of the Palestinian population. Motivated by the twin impulses of expansionism and exclusivism, Israeli actions since the June War have aimed at the exploitation of the physical and human resources of the West Bank and the Gaza Strip. In their totality, these actions constitute an attack on the very soul and structure of the Palestinian society. It was not sufficient to expropriate the land; it was also important to dismantle the social, economic and cultural structures that gave the Palestinians any sense of national identity or consciousness.

Israel's settlement policy has resulted not only in the expropriation of Palestinian land but also in the stifling of economic development and growth in the land which was not expropriated. The West Bank and the

---

[1] February 19, 1982.

Gaza Strip economies have been rurally based, with agriculture accounting for the highest proportion of productive output and of employment. When their lands were not expropriated to make room for new Jewish settlements, Palestinian farmers were given little access to scarce water resources, thus making it difficult for them to cultivate their farmlands. Of the 331 artesian wells in the West Bank, some 20 wells have been drilled by the Israelis to service the needs of the newly established Jewish settlements; yet in 1978, the total volume of water discharged from 314 Palestinian wells amounted to 33 million cubic metres, whereas in the same time period, the 17 Israeli wells discharged over 14 million cubic metres. It is now estimated that Palestinian farmers receive no more than one-sixth of the water available to them. As a consequence of water control and exploitation, Palestinian employment in the agricultural sector has declined significantly, both on the West Bank and more seriously in the Gaza Strip.

Of those Palestinians who continued to work in agriculture, many found it more profitable to do so on the farms of the new Israeli landowners, often at wages averaging about 40 percent of those paid to their Israeli counterparts. In this manner, Palestinian farmers have become an underpaid and exploited labour force on the very lands from which they had been expelled. But the change in traditional work patterns was far more pervasive. The stifling of economic growth and development in their lands, in their towns and in their villages made Palestinian workers reluctant partners in the exploitation of their labour by the Israelis. Palestinian workers were prepared to take semi-skilled and unskilled jobs that Israeli workers were not prepared to accept: jobs in unskilled construction and agriculture, cleaning, restaurant work, garbage disposal, etc. The total number of employed Gaza Palestinians who work in Israel has risen from 10 percent in 1970 to 43 percent in the early 1980's, and in the West Bank from 12 percent to 30 percent in the same time period. Almost half of the employed men and women of the Occupied Territories now work for Israelis.

Palestinians working for Israelis are not allowed to belong to the Histadrut (Israel's Trade Union Federation) nor are they allowed to form their own unions. As a result, they are totally at the mercy of their employers. They are paid inferior wages, denied fringe benefits, and may be dismissed without notice. Deductions amounting to almost $2 billion have been taken from their wages, however, to help finance Histadrut benefit schemes available only to Israeli citizens. They are not allowed to stay in Israeli cities and towns overnight. Everyday, they have to spend numerous hours commuting to their places of work, but must return in the evening to their homes in the Occupied Territories.

It is sometimes argued by Israeli officials that the material conditions of the residents of the West Bank and Gaza have improved during Israel's twenty years of occupation. This is partially true. Palestinians do seem to have more spending power. In the 1970's, this was largely due to remittances received from relatives working in the then economically booming Arabian Gulf countries. But the increase in living standards also came from the provision of cheap labour to the Israelis. In neither case, however, was there an increase in the productive output at home. As a result, the economy of the West Bank has become completely dependent on structural forces outside its control. In the 1970's, for example, when Israel experienced a recession, it was the Palestinian workers who were the first to suffer.

In addition to the exploitation of the physical and human resources of the Occupied Territories, occupation has had a pernicious effect on the daily lives of the Palestinian inhabitants. They have been constantly subjected to harassment, intimidation and flagrant violations of their human rights, all with very little protection from the law.

The Occupied Territories operate under a military administration. The Israeli authorities pick and choose from a whole variety of antiquated, but convenient, laws and regulations to give legal validity to their actions. They have used Ottoman law dating back to the 18th century; they have enforced the British Emergency Regulations used by the British in Palestine prior to the establishment of the Israeli State; they have even made selective use of Jordanian law even though they do not recognize Jordan's sovereignty over the West Bank. And, when no laws can be made use of, a decree or an order by the military governor gives a legal basis for any action or measure. Over 1800 such military orders have been enunciated so far.

Israeli authorities have used these regulations, laws and military pronouncements to undertake actions which have received the condemnation of the world community. Israel has expropriated over 50 percent of the land it had conquered. Much of the land taken over by the Israelis was 'state land' claimed by Jordan. Under the Jordanian government, 'state land', though technically belonging to the state, was left to be used by its occupants and could be passed by inheritance to their heirs but could not be sold without permission of the government. Article 55 of the Hague Regulations specifically states that 'state land' does not become the property of the occupying power; Articles 47 and 49 of the Fourth Geneva Convention also prohibit "annexation in whole or in part" of occupied territory and forbid an occupying power 'from deporting or transferring any of its civilian population to the occupied territories', respectively. In contravention of these international rules regulating the duties and rights of the occupier, Israel has both expropriated the land and created over 130 Jewish settlements on it. By 1987, there were some 70,000 Jewish colonists living in the West Bank, and somewhat more than 2,000 in the 30 percent of the Gaza Strip expropriated for them. Sixty percent of the best farmland in those areas has been seized from Palestinians. Using the British Emergency Regulations, Israeli authorities have sometimes declared private property "restricted for security reasons"; access to that land by its rightful Palestinian owner is then forbidden. Having denied the Palestinian farmer access to the land presumably for three years, the military administrator, using Jordanian law, declares it 'state land' and promptly makes it available for further Jewish settlement.

Palestinians residing in the Occupied Territories have also had to face brutal violations of their human rights. Contrary to Article 49 of the Fourth Geneva Convention which forbids the deportation of civilians to any other country, Israel has in its twenty years of occupation deported almost 2000 Palestinians, accusing them of 'agitation', 'membership in an illegal organization' (i.e., in some member organization of the Palestine Liberation Organization), and 'terrorist activities'. For the most part, the deportees have been educated professionals and political leaders, including several elected mayors whose activities were deemed hostile to the Israeli military occupation. In this manner, the emergence of any type of Palestinian political leadership has been undermined and the fear of separation from family and land instilled in those who might otherwise engage in political activity.

Palestinians have also been subjected to collective punishment, mostly undertaken without court proceedings and without regard to the rights of the innocent. Families have had their houses blown up as punishment for alleged 'terroristic' crimes by a member of the family. Over 1200 houses have been destroyed in this manner. Other forms of collective punishment have included the following: the imposition of lengthy curfews on cities, villages and camps, the closing of universities, travel restrictions, the closing down of businesses, and the harassment of innocent civilians. These actions are in clear violation of the Fourth Geneva Convention. Article 33 prohibits the punishment of civilians for crimes they have not personally committed, and Article 53 prohibits the destruction of property except when such destruction is for military reasons. Israeli authorities justify collective punishment by appealing to the antiquated British Emergency Regulations, though the validity of such an appeal has not been accepted by the international community. The Fourth Geneva Convention, of which Israel is a signatory, overrides any state legislation which is contrary to its letter.

The Israeli authorities have also made extensive use of administrative detention and arbitrary arrest. The old British Emergency Regulations allowed for the detention of people suspected of security offenses for periods up to six months without due process of law. This practice was used by the Israeli authorities until 1979 when it was formally discontinued as a result of condemnation by various international bodies, including Amnesty International and the United Nations. Nevertheless, Palestinians are still subjected to a less severe form of administrative detention. Any Palestinian suspected of a security violation, including stone-throwing, 'incitement', raising the Palestinian flag, singing Palestinian patriotic songs in public and distributing proscribed literature, may be detained for a period of 18 days, and sometimes more, without charges and without contact with family or attorneys. In fact, any Israeli soldier may detain any Palestinian if the soldier has "grounds for suspicion" that the Palestinian has committed an offense.

It is estimated that almost 250,000 West Bank Palestinians, one out of five, have experienced some form of imprisonment during the twenty years of occupation, even if the imprisonment was for a short period of time. The Israeli authorities use detention not only to punish people for alleged security offenses but also as scare tactics to influence the prisoner's political orientation or that of his friends and family.

Since prisoners are held in detention without necessarily being charged with a specific offense, an attempt is made to extract a confession through the use of harsh interrogation techniques. Interrogation normally takes place in the first two weeks of detainment, long before observers from the International Committee for the Red Cross or attorneys may see the prisoner. Some detainees have been suspended by the hands, burnt with cigarette stubs, beaten on the genitals with rods, tied up and blindfolded for days, received electric shocks to the temples, the mouth, the chest and the testicles. The use of torture has been documented by various international bodies. An investigation by the London Sunday Times in 1977 revealed that Palestinian prisoners are subjected to widespread and systematic torture. A report by the National Lawyers Guild of the U.S. came to the same conclusion, and more recently, Israel's own commission of inquiry, the Landau Commission, confirmed that Palestinians living in Israel and the Occupied Territories have been subjected to torture during interrogation by the Shin Beth. And while the Commission recommended that torture not be used against Israeli Palestinians, it was more sympathetic towards the use of 'moderate' physical violence against Palestinian detainees from the West Bank and Gaza.

But even when Palestinian residents of the West Bank and the Gaza Strip have not experienced the 'iron fist' of the Israeli occupiers first hand, they all live under conditions of fear, anxiety and turmoil. The average Palestinian encounters the Israeli, not as another human being, but as a soldier with limitless power over him, as a settler determined to take his land and as an occupier who can imprison his children, close down his schools and even kill him. The conduct of the Israeli authorities in the Occupied Territories over the twenty years of occupation has done very little to dispel these fears.

THE INTIFADA

James A. Graff and Farid Ohan

December 9th, 1987 marks the beginning of the Palestinian Intifada, the mass uprising of Palestinians who had endured twenty years of life under Israeli occupation on the West Bank and in the Gaza Strip. One of the meanings of the Arabic word, "intifada", is "shaking off": the aim of the Intifada is to shake off the yoke of Israeli occupation and to establish an independent Palestinian state on the West Bank and in Gaza. The 1967 War left close to a million Palestinians under repressive Israeli military occupation. The occupier was bent on transforming every aspect of the society it had come to occupy so as to negate the Palestinians' existence as a people, dismantle their social, political and economic institutions, confiscate their land and exploit their human and natural resources. For the occupier, the Arab inhabitants were seen as an obstacle to their efforts to "reclaim" what they define as the historic land of Israel. To overcome this "obstacle", the Israeli government proceeded to confiscate Palestinian land (60% of the West Bank and over 40% of Gaza); they diverted water, making it impossible for many Palestinians to farm their lands; they periodically closed educational institutions, disrupting and weakening the education of Palestinian children and youth; they forbade the teaching of Palestinian history; they dismantled political, social and cultural institutions so that Palestinians might lose their sense of identity. They supported collaborators and brutally put down any resistance to occupation. They fostered conflict among Palestinians belonging to different religious and political factions. They exploited Palestinian labourers, relegating them to menial and unskilled jobs while paying them wages much inferior to those paid to their Israeli counterparts. They tried to create a state of economic dependency based on a relationship of fear and oppression.

For a while, this strategy of control and colonization worked. The Israelis reaped all the benefits of occupation, but few of its costs. They established new settlements on the best Palestinian land; they kept the occupied population under control with minimal effort and, in fact, at a profit. They found a new market for their goods and services. The Palestinian inhabitants, who were yet to grasp the full dimensions of the catastrophe that had befallen them, initially caved in under Israeli tactics. They lived from day to day, hoping that the Arab World would come to their rescue and that the international community would not permit the occupation to continue. But the Camp David Accord (1978), which gave no role to Palestinians in determining their future, and the Israeli invasion of Lebanon in 1982, with the further dispersion of PLO forces and increased repression in the Occupied Territories, made it clear that there would be no military rescue by Arab states, and that the international community was powerless to end the occupation so long as the United States accepted it. The Palestinians had gradually come to the realization that only through their own action could they bring about a change in their situation, which had deteriorated to an intolerable point. They saw themselves on the verge of total and irreversible dependence, and cultural and social annihilation as a people.

Like mass uprisings elsewhere, the Intifada is an expression of the universal human inclination to fight oppression, injustice, brutality and the denial of basic human, religious and national rights. For the Palestinians, the Intifada represents an affirmation of themselves as a people, a negation of their subjugation under occupation, and an assertion of their right to live in an independent state under a leadership of their own choosing.

The Intifada Begins

There always seems to be a single incident which precipitates major historical events. On December 8, 1987, four Palestinians were crushed to death and seven others seriously injured when an Israeli military truck crushed their cars at the checkpoint leading from Gaza to Israel. The driver of the transport was the brother of an Israeli stabbed to death in Gaza City two days before. The Israelis claimed the incident to be a traffic accident. The Palestinians in Gaza saw it as a revenge murder. The next day there were demonstrations in Gaza in which 15 year-old Hatem Sissi from Jabalya Refugee Camp was shot in the heart. Within days, there were demonstrations on the West Bank in which other teenagers were killed. There had been demonstrations before, and there had been killings of Palestinians, especially in the previous year, and before that in 1982 during the Invasion of Lebanon, but they had been largely confined to particular regions, towns or refugee camps. Now, the demonstrations spread throughout the major centres of the Occupied Territories. The general attitude, especially among the youth in the camps, now was: "They can do no more than kill us." Thus was the barrier of fear broken and thus began the Intifada.

Although there had been numerous demonstrations and strikes during the previous twenty years protesting the occupation or responding to specific repressive measures, there had never been a concerted and sustained uprising. A concerted uprising requires a developed infrastructure of local and regional organizations, a leadership to direct it, and discipline to carry it out. An infrastructure of popular committees focusing on medical relief, education, women's concerns, agricultural development, the organization of labourers and merchants, students and professionals -- all this had evolved since the mid-'70's in an effort to address the variety of needs of the Palestinians under occupation. These popular committees coordinated the local committees in the various towns, villages and camps into a network.

After the seizure of the West Bank and the Gaza Strip, the Israeli authorities, using the Jordanian secret police files, exiled nearly 1200 Palestinian community leaders, including university teachers, doctors, lawyers, student leaders, unionists and journalists. What now gradually emerged, however, was a new underground leadership, many of them student leaders, also schooled in the brutal conditions of Israeli prisons where they had been detained for political activities. This new national leadership of the Intifada has brought with it new ideas, methods and organizational skills. Although in the beginning the Intifada was spontaneous, it soon took the form of a disciplined popular uprising with clear objectives and a well-defined strategy. By December 21, they were able to call the first Palestinian general strike since 1939.

Major objectives were to lessen Palestinian economic dependence on Israel by encouraging Palestinian "self-sufficiency" and boycotts of Israeli goods, and to demonstrate Palestinian control over their own economy by determining their hours of business in defiance of the military authorities. Another aim was to demonstrate Palestinian determination to resist further Israeli economic exploitation, and thus induce them to reconsider the wisdom of continuing the occupation. The national leadership of the Intifada started issuing circulars giving instructions regarding business hours, strikes, marches (such as that of Palestinian women on International Women's Day), showing the Palestinian flag, etc. The Israeli authorities tried, without success, to fake these circulars.

Popular committees, which included representatives of the major political factions and all strata of the local Palestinian communities, sprang up at the grass-roots level to handle local affairs. Different sections of refugee camps and towns, for example, have their own popular committees. The membership is secret -- the Israeli authorities have outlawed them and have threatened to expel or to imprison for ten years anyone active in them, such as in teaching children (the schools in the West Bank and the Gaza Strip were closed for almost all of 1988). These popular committees, in effect, form the grass-roots Palestinian parallel government in the Israeli-occupied territories. They have helped organize the distribution of food when the local community has been under siege. They have provided classes for children whose schools have been closed and medical relief for those beaten or shot by Israeli troops. They have organized patrols to warn of the approach of Israeli army contingents or settlers. The popular organizations which were in place by December 1987 made the Intifada possible; the local popular committees which developed in the early stages of the Intifada have kept it going.

The Intifada has had a democratizing and unifying effect on the Palestinians. The internal dissent and rivalry, and the traditional undemocratic leadership styles which characterized an earlier period of their history have now given way to a highly united, democratized mass struggle.

Stones and Flags

The Children of the Stones, mostly teen-age and younger, have become the symbols of the Intifada. The TV-viewer's image of the Intifada is one of children throwing stones at heavily-armed Israeli troops who retaliate with tear gas, rubber bullets (metal slugs encased in hard rubber), live ammunition and savage beatings. These scenes are repeated daily in different places when Israeli troops raid a town or a village, or stand guard at the sealed entrances of refugee camps, towns or villages to which they are laying siege. The routine of troops arriving to confront a crowd of youngsters, or a crowd of youngsters arriving to confront troops, has been repeated daily. The troops usually lay down a barrage of asphyxiating gas -- a new variety produced in Salzburg, Pennsylvania, which causes severe abdominal pains, headache, choking and suffocation in confined spaces. This is usually followed by volleys of rubber bullets, fired thirteen at a time from a cannister which fits on the barrel of a rifle. The troops all too often fire live ammunition with the rubber bullets -- sometimes in the air, sometimes into the crowd. Sometimes they start with live ammunition. In a typical confrontation, the youngsters will advance in groups, some carrying the Palestinian flag, others hurling rocks: the troops will retreat to a safe distance, and then advance as the kids retreat for more ammunition. Then the shooting starts, and finally, if the lines of children break, the troops rush in with clubs, beating whomever they can lay their hands on. As a rule, the children they catch are continuously beaten, sometimes tied to trees and beaten, beaten in army trucks, in jeeps and in buses which haul them off for detention where they are beaten again.

Images of Israeli soldiers beating youngsters are also associated with the Intifada. What TV viewers have not seen has been the systematic, house-by-house beatings of men, women and children of all ages in refugee camps and villages. Nor have viewers seen Israeli troops fire gas cannisters into homes, blanketing entire sections of camps or towns with the choking gas, firing their rubber bullets at people inside their own homes, or in narrow alleyways in camps, forcing children to lie in open sewers as they beat and kick them. The oldest victim was 102, beaten twice; the youngest, an infant in his mother's arms, was beaten with a club intended for both. The "Children of the Stones" have not been deterred -- if anything, Israeli brutality has strengthened their resolve.

The Israeli Responses to the Intifada

The Israeli government miscalculated the nature of what confronted them in mid-December, 1987. They believed that they could easily suppress the spreading demonstrations by applying once again, the "Iron Fist Policy". They were blind to the transformations which had occurred in the psyche and social structures of the Palestinians. They had underestimated the Palestinians' resolve to live in dignity, on their own land, and in the political and social manner of their choosing. They thought that they could re-establish control through fear, but more and more Palestinians, especially youths and children, are losing their fear, as anger and determination to resist the occupation grow with each repressive measure.

From December 9, 1987 until January 15, 1988, Israeli troops shot 40 Palestinians to death, mainly teenagers. During the same period, 14 people died from gas, half of them infants asphyxiated when gas cannisters were shot into their homes. Several hundred were wounded during that period, and thousands more injured by beatings. The international outcry against the shootings led Defense Minister Yitzhak Rabin to announce a new policy of beatings. From January 16 until February 1st, the Israel Defence Force managed not to kill a single Palestinian by gunfire. Western viewers then saw on their TV screens Israeli troops smashing children's hands with rifle butts, stones and clubs.

Systematic mass beatings had actually started early in January and continued well into the next month. Embarrassed by international reaction, the Israeli Government authorized local commanders to declare the areas in which they were operating "military zones" closed to journalists. At the same time, they resumed the policy of using live ammunition. When in early March, 1988, Rabin announced that any Palestinian suspected of carrying or of having thrown a molotov cocktail might be shot, the number of shooting deaths rose markedly. On April 16, an Israeli assassination squad murdered Abu Jihad, the PLO official with responsibility for overseeing PLO operations connected with the Intifada.

The use of tear gas by Israeli troops in enclosed spaces was responsible for a large number of miscarriages. Although we do not have accurate statistics on the number of miscarriages in hospitals, let alone those unreported on the outside, the totals for 1988 are estimated to be in the hundreds. On two nights in Gaza alone, 23 women who had been subjected to the gas miscarried in hospital. The gas has been fired into hospitals by raiding Israeli troops, usually entering to arrest youngsters using hospitals as sanctuaries, or to arrest the wounded, sometimes beating them in their beds, or while taking them for interrogation.

Reference has been made to the use by the IDF of siege tactics against Palestinian villages and camps, during which their food and water supplies have been cut off for as long as several weeks at a time. From May onward through the summer and fall, over 100,000 fruit and olive trees of the Palestinians were uprooted and several hundred thousand seedlings destroyed by the IDF and Jewish settlers, in an attempt to weaken Palestinian agriculture and their capacity to feed themselves.

Collective punishment, illegal under international law, came into use again against the Intifada. By the end of 1988, 184 Palestinian homes had been totally or partially demolished, totally or partially sealed. In addition, 363 homes had been demolished on the grounds that they had been built without licences. These demolitions were widely viewed by Palestinians as punitive, because such licences are almost impossible to secure.

To accommodate the more than 5000 Palestinians held under administrative detention (detention without charges or trial) out of the 30,000 arrested, of whom roughly 1,000 have been women, the Israeli government has established six new official detention centres. The most notorious are Ansar III (Kitziot) in the Negev Desert and Dhahariyya, near Hebron, where the detainees suffer from gross overcrowding, are routinely beaten and humiliated, and are denied adequate food, water and medical care. Since prisoners are often moved from one detention centre to another, most families learn of the whereabouts of a detained relative only from others who have been released. There is no systematic effort to let the family know whether a husband, a son or brother has been arrested.

The Israeli government has increasingly resorted to the extreme measure of "deportation" (exile). Thirty-two persons were expelled in 1988, despite repeated condemnations of the practice by the UN Security Council and protests even from the U.S. government.

The Israeli government has also closed every Palestinian labour union office, the offices of the West Bank Physicians' Union and its clinic, illegalized every popular committee, kept all universities closed throughout 1988, closed every major Palestinian charitable organization, and cut telephone links between the outside world and the Occupied Territories.

In its effort to suppress the Intifada, the Israeli government has, in effect, broadened its attacks on the Palestinians to encompass every major Palestinian institution. The economic effects of these measures for the Palestinians have been damaging. Deteriorating health conditions and malnutrition, already a problem in the refugee camps of Gaza, have worsened. Of the estimated 46,000 Palestinians seriously injured by Israeli troops and settlers during 1988, most have received inadequate medical attention, often for fear of being arrested in Israeli-controlled government hospitals. Thousands of acres of farmland have been torched or bulldozed; crops have rotted while farmers have been prevented by force from harvesting them. Despite this, the Intifada continues: independence has its price in blood and treasure. (See Appendix at end of article.)

The Cost to Israel

Before the Intifada, Israel annually sold over $1 billion U.S. in goods and services to the Occupied Territories, largely in textiles, construction materials, food and clothing, accounting for 10% of all Israeli exports. That figure has been halved because of Palestinian emphasis on economic self-sufficiency, and the drop in Palestinian purchasing power. Economic sectors dependent on cheap Palestinian labour have been especially hard-hit. Over 100,000 Palestinians from the Territories formerly worked in Israel, but tens of thousands have stopped showing up since the Intifada began. In agriculture, tons of Israeli citrus fruit have rotted on the trees. There has been a drop of between 10-15%

in construction because Palestinian workers have remained in the Territories. According to the U.S. Embassy in Israel, the direct military and police costs of suppressing the Intifada have averaged $120 million per month and another $38 million in indirect costs, for a total of nearly $2 billion in 1988. If we add the Jerusalem Post estimate of a $350,000,000 loss in revenue from tourism and a $500,000,000 loss in exports to the Occupied Territories, the grand total comes to about $2.8 billion. If the U.S. were to pick up three quarters of the extra cost, as it did after Israel's invasion of Lebanon, it would have to add an extra $2 billion to its annual aid to Israel of $4 billion. Certainly, the cost to Israel of trying to smash the Intifada has added to the woes of an already troubled economy.

The human costs to Israel are not so easily reckoned, nor can they be easily covered by a generous United States. What young Israeli soldiers have been required to do to unarmed Palestinians is both brutalizing and demoralizing. The Israeli government has been sufficiently concerned about low morale to send special teams of army psychiatrists to counsel their troops. The full social costs have yet to be seen. By the end of 1988, over three hundred Israeli Reserve Officers had refused to serve in the Occupied Territories. Many are members of Yesh Gavul ("There is a limit/border"), over 200 of whom have been sentenced to serve 1-3 months in military prisons for refusing, on grounds of conscience, to serve in the Territories. One reservist, Adam Keller, served six months in prison for painting "End the Occupation" and "Yesh Gavul" on some 140 military vehicles. By contrast, three soldiers convicted of burying four Palestinian youths alive received two to three month prison sentences. Retired Israeli Colonel, Dov Yirmiya, 68, who refused to obey orders to fire on children in Lebanon, was charged with inciting disobedience because, since the beginning of the uprising, he has urged young Israelis of conscience not to serve in the Occupied Territories. He could face up to 15 years imprisonment, if convicted.

Israelis have been polarized by the Intifada and especially by their government's "Iron Fist Policy". There has been a shift to the right, and the number of those who favour mass expulsion of Palestinians from the Territories has increased to 40%. There has also been an increase among those who are prepared to withdraw from the Territories and to negotiate a settlement. The shift towards negotiations and withdrawal, however, is significant because of the major figures who have changed their views, not because of their number. The Intifada made Israeli-Palestinian relations the key issue of the elections which resulted in a slight right-wing (Likud) edge over the Labour position. Labour had supported a largely ceremonial UN-sponsored conference, negotiations with Jordan over the disposition of the Territories, aimed at retaining at least 40% of the West Bank. Likud has steadfastly refused to surrender one inch of conquered territory. Both have refused to negotiate with the PLO and have rejected an independent Palestinian state. Parties supporting negotiations and withdrawal have retained, overall, roughly the number of seats they held in the Knesset before the election, while religious parties, old and new, have gained. Only one of the religious parties has a clear position on the Territories, urging mass expulsions. The others are concerned primarily to insure that Orthodox Judaism's tenets be enshrined in law.

Although there is strong support among Israeli Arabs for the aims and objectives of the Intifada, this support was not clearly visible in their voting pattern in the last election. About 10,000 votes were cast for Likud, for instance. Arab clan leaders were able to deliver votes on promises of privileges from Likud and Labour organizers, such as halting the demolition of homes built without licences. (However, after the election, houses were demolished in several Palestinian towns within Israel proper.) The Arab vote was split, too, by personal rivalries and ideological factionalism and some may have mistakenly voted for the wrong party.

Although there have been stone-throwing incidents and even fire-bombings of vehicles with molotov cocktails in Israel proper, and although some Palestinian citizens of Israel have been placed under administrative detention, Israeli Arabs have not taken up the Intifada. This is in part because of fear of Jewish Israeli reprisals and of the re-imposition of martial law, to which they were subjected for 16 years in the Galilee after the Israeli conquest of 1948. It is due also to the efforts of the older, established leadership to keep those who want to be more active under control, and to their acceptance of their status of citizens, albeit second- or third-class citizens within Israel. They are not under military occupation, nor are they daily subjected to the humiliations and brutality suffered by their cousins in the West Bank and Gaza. For them, there is still a hope that, ultimately, the democracy which Jews still enjoy in Israel will be increasingly extended to them. They recognize that, as a minority, they could be smashed and expelled if they caused trouble. Those in the Occupied Territories know that Israel would not extend the franchise to them in any meaningful way without, in the long run, jeopardizing Jewish Israeli privilege and Jewish Israeli control. Their experience with the Israelis has made them adamant about independence.

It has also forced them to develop their own institutions and to rebel in order to preserve their culture and integrity as a distinct people.

Israel's brutal measures to crush the Intifada have turned public sympathies in Western Europe and North America toward the Palestinians, resulting in the increasing isolation of Israel and the United States at the international level. A two-state solution had been the PLO's objective since the mid-seventies, but it was the insistence of the Intifada on an independent Palestinian State side-by-side with Israel that forced the PLO to pass a vote supporting this objective in its parliament, the Palestine National Council, and to declare the formation of a Palestinian State on November 15, 1988. This entailed the recognition of Israel's right to exist along side such a Palestinian state, and the right of all states in the region to exist in peace within secure borders. It also meant the acceptance of UN Resolutions 242 and 338 as the basis for an international peace conference. Furthermore, although the PLO had previously condemned terrorism, that is attacks on civilian targets, they again -- in response to American demands -- condemned the use of terrorism in all its forms. In an historic vote at the United Nations on December 15, 1988, following Chairman Arafat's address before the General Assembly, convened to hear him in Geneva because the U.S. had denied him a visa to attend the UN session in New York, every country of the world except the United States, Israel, Canada and Costa Rica supported the call for an international peace conference on the Middle East. The U.S. and Israel voted against the resolution, while Canada and Costa Rica abstained. Israel was further isolated and chagrined by the United States' agreement the day before this vote to direct talks with the PLO on "substantive issues". Within days, the stalemate of the Israeli November election was broken when a Likud-Labour coalition was formed -- still rejecting any negotiations with the PLO. Meanwhile, the killing of Palestinians has increased.

The Israeli heavy-handed attempt to repress the Intifada had not only caused a major division within Jewish Zionist communities (the majority) in North America, but has also to some degree weakened Christian Zionist support. Christians Zionists fall into two broad camps: those who accept the biblical right of the Jewish people to a homeland in Palestine and who feel guilty (and rightly so) about Christian silence and inaction when European Jews were being murdered en masse by the Nazis; and then those who interpret the prophecies of the Book of Revelation as requiring the setting up of the State of Israel as a necessary stage for the conversion of the Jews, the destruction of the present world system and the return of Jesus to establish God's kingdom on Earth.

Though there has been little weakening of such views, there has been some softening of attitudes among the guilt-ridden because of the growing recognition that silence over the injustices inflicted on the Palestinians is no more justifiable than silence over the fate of European Jewry. For them, the myth that a suffering people cannot inflict suffering on another has been shattered, and the barrier against moral reproach breached. It is now permissible to raise the issue of Palestinian rights in North American churches. Israeli repression aimed at the <u>Intifada</u> has also legitimized public criticism of Israel, even in the media, and has freed journalists, who had previously been cowed by the Israel lobby into silence, to speak. The more who speak openly, the more difficult it is to silence them again. Israeli handling of the Intifada has been a series of miscalculations, underestimating the will and capacity of the Palestinians, over-estimating the Lobby's power to silence the media and keep Western public opinion in line.

Conclusion

At this point, the Israeli government is isolated, confronted by an increasingly polarized society, with heavy debts and a flagging economy. It may resort to the myth of Massada where Jewish extremists committed mass suicide rather than surrender to Roman troops, or to the myth of Samson destroying himself and his enemies, by bringing their house down upon them all. It might, on the other hand, finally accept a negotiated settlement requiring withdrawal from the Occupied Territories. That, however, would require a consensus that the Land of Israel is mainly the territory held before 1967, that world Jewry cannot and need not almost all reside in Israel, and that Israel is, after all, the state, not of the Jews of the world, but of its citizens, Palestinian and Jewish, including both European and Arab Jews. Which course is chosen depends very much on the United States. The option of mass expulsion would require another war -- the United States may not want such a war. The only other real option is for Israel to negotiate withdrawal. Which option she will take remains an open question at this point.

THE WOMEN OF PALESTINE

Ghada Talhami

Palestinian women have always played an active role in the Palestinian national movement. Their activism dates back to the early phase of the national struggle when the major demands of the Palestinians were the cancellation of the Balfour Declaration and an end to the mistreatment of Palestinian prisoners in British jails. The women led a separate struggle of their own which paralleled the formal movement but did not necessarily integrate the women's actions with the men's. Separate all-female demonstrations, where veiled women were a visible phenomenon, and separate female organizations characterized the early phase of 1920 to 1948. Among the earliest of these organizations was the Palestine Women's Union which was founded in 1921 by Muslim and Christian women.[1] Through this organization, efforts were make to link up with other Arab feminist organizations in an effort to publicize the Palestinian struggle and gain support for it among various progressive sectors of the Arab World. This strategy proved to be a resounding success when the Eastern Women's Congress convened in Cairo in 1938 and adopted a set of resolutions endorsing the Palestinian struggle against the British Mandate authorities and the unrestricted influx of Zionist settlers to the Palestinian homeland. This Congress convened under the leadership of Huda Sha'rawi, President of the Egyptian Feminist Union and the most renowned Arab feminist of her day, and succeeded in publicizing the plight of the Arabs of Palestine and in placing the issue before the international and Egyptian publics.[2]

Military participation on the part of Palestinian women in the Arab-Jewish War of 1948 was sporadic and limited. Much of this had to do with the class-origin of the early wave of Palestinian feminists. Since most of these women came from the well-to-do classes who had the necessary leisure to pursue liberationist and feminist goals, the likelihood of involvement in the military aspect of the struggle was limited. Indeed, the only incidents of their genuine participation in the armed struggle

---

[1]General Union of Palestinian Women, From the Palestinian Women's Struggle (Beirut: n.d.), p. 4. See also: Matiel E.T. Mogannem, The Arab Woman and the Palestine Problem (London: Herbert Joseph, 1937), passim.

[2]Amaal K.B. al-Subki, Al-Harakat al-nisa'iyyah fi Misr (The Feminist Movement in Egypt) (Cairo: al-Hay'ah al-Misriyah lil-Kitab, 1986), pp. 81-86.

materialized during the 1936 Revolt and were by peasant women. Most of the women enrolled in feminist organizations at the time devoted themselves to support activities such as collecting food and sheltering the children of the 'martyrs' (that is those who were killed in the Revolt).[1] Thus, by 1948, Palestinian feminism was still limited both by its class origins and the extent of its role within the national movement.

The beginning of the Palestinian diaspora in 1948 also inadvertently intensified the politicization of women of all classes. This was particularly the case in the harsh refugee camps throughout the Arab World, where the traditional, peasant Palestinian family was subjected to tremendous pressures. In many instances, women became bread-winners under extremely unfavorable socio-economic conditions, often having to make do with whatever unskilled work became available. Due to the large migration of working-age men to the new employment opportunities in the Persian Gulf oil-countries, women became heads of households. It was no surprise that when the Palestinian Liberation Organization began to mobilize the population of the Jordanian, Syrian and Lebanese refugee camps, the women proved to be eager recruits. Women's participation in the civilian structure of the PLO in Lebanon was particularly extensive. The Palestine Red Crescent Society, the educational institutions, as well as the PLO's huge economic cooperative, SAMED, were heavily staffed by women. Women also participated in military decision-making in the refugee camps of Southern Lebanon where the proximity of the Israeli border transformed these camps into frontier military outposts. More significantly, the women were now organized into the General Union of Palestinian Women, a recognized cadre within the structure of the PLO. This organization was given representation within the Palestine National Council, the Palestinians' parliament in exile. Between one and three women were now included within the PLO's Central Committee. Undoubtedly, the Palestinians' Lebanon experience consolidated feminist gains in the political sphere.[2]

Inevitably, the Palestinian diaspora of 1948 produced a fragmented society with varying degrees of transformation. The military defeat of 1967 and the imposition of Israeli military rule over a large segment of the Palestinian population in the West Bank and Gaza produced structural changes in the pattern of Palestinian feminist organizations and radical

---

[1]G. Talhami, "Women in the Movement: Their Long, Uncelebrated History," Al-Fajr (May 30, 1986), passim.

[2]Ingela Bendt and James Downing, We Shall Return: Women of Palestine, Ann Henning trans. (London: Zed press. 1982), pp. 16-17, 78.

changes in the overall societal role of women. Not only did the old-style social-welfare organizations led by women become instantly nationalist and activist, but a new type of women's organizations emerged specifically to serve the needs of the female working population. Profound economic, as well as political changes were transforming the occupied population. Increasing Palestinian dependence on the industrialized Israeli society became clearly an objective of the Israeli military authorities. The West Bank and Gaza were speedily converted into a captive market for Israeli manufactured goods, and, more significantly for Palestinian women, they became a source of cheap labor. For the first time in the history of the West Bank and Gaza, women became a proletariat in a typical colonial setting where their labor was exploited without the benefit of protective labor laws or freely-operating unions. Moreover, women increasingly became managers of their families because of the harshness of Israeli laws which thinned out the ranks of males through imprisonment or expulsion.[1]

The social-welfare agencies, run entirely by women, became dedicated to the national effort by providing free schooling and boarding facilities for the children of prisoners and martyrs and by providing training programs for unskilled women. Societies, such as In'ash al-Usra (The Reanimation of the Family) in al-Bireh, led this effort with a certain master-plan in mind. By recognizing that unskilled Palestinian women were destined to swell the ranks of the most exploited sector of the Israeli economy, In'ash al-Usra specifically taught skills such as food-processing, embroidery, and the like, which can lead to self-employment under benign conditions. For those women who did join the ranks of migrant Palestinian labor, bussed daily to Israeli industrial centers, or the women who worked at home on consignment basis for Israeli businessmen, a new organized effort was needed. This situation was eventually addressed through the emergence of Women's Work Committees, which sprouted in every major urban center and refugee camp. These committees, which attracted younger and highly politicized women, made a genuine effort to prepare working women for the realities of the Israeli economic policies towards the occupied population. Providing low-cost nursery schools became a top priority, as well as educating the women about their union and economic rights. The post-1967 experience in the West Bank and Gaza, therefore, provided valuable

---

[1]Joseph Algazy, "Workers in the Occupied Territories," New Outlook, vol. 28, no. 4 (April, 1985), p. 17; "UN Documents Hardships Facing Palestinian Women," Al-Fajr (July 12, 1985), pp. 9-11.

experience of work under the harsh climate of the occupation. The new roles charted for women turned out to be constructive and necessary for the survival of Palestinian society.[1]

In some respects, the experience of economic and political domination by the Israelis proved devastating for Palestinian male-female relations. To those Palestinian males fully conscious of the historic continuity of the women's struggle and their contribution to the national cause, female activism in the 1970's was a positive phenomenon. Generally speaking, Palestinian males under occupation recognized the constructive aspects of the women's roles. Even as they became subjected to harsh prison conditions and sexual threats and harassment at the hands of the enemy, most Palestinian women were not discouraged from taking part in resistance activities to the occupation. A certain sector of the Palestinian male population, however, felt threatened by this activism and its implications for the traditional pattern of male-female relations. Palestinian men who were themselves victimized by Israeli racism and economic exploitation through their work experience proved to be intolerant of female activism. In the Gaza camps, in particular, loss of male dignity through negative work experiences produced despondency and an acute sense of threat to their traditional male role. In many instances, this resulted in a strong desire to return to old values and old social norms. Gaza women interviewed just prior to the Intifada seem fully aware of the causes and significance of this phenomenon and fully prepared to deal with it.[2]

Since 1967, and with the launching of the PLO as the representative leadership of the Palestinian people, Palestinian women have surged forward to gain international recognition for their cause. Official Palestinian delegations participated in all major UN End of Decade Conferences on Women, in Mexico City, Copenhagen, and in Nairobi. In all of these conferences, Palestinian women articulated the harsh conditions of national dismemberment and life under the occupation. They emerged as the most visible example of a society victimized by settler colonialism where women and children become the innocent casualties of international conflicts. No feminist group could deny the brutal circumstances surrounding Palestinian women, nor the impact of settler colonialism on the Palestinian family. Western feminists, particularly mainstream United States feminist organizations, however,

---

[1]"Palestinian Women's Committees," Al-Fajr (March 21, 1984), passim.

[2]Paul Cossali and Clive Robson, Stateless in Gaza (London: Zed Press, 1986), pp. 38-39.

became vehicles for the interjection of Zionist rhetoric into these conferences. The cause of international feminist solidarity became mired in the tangled web of Zionist and Palestinian claims and counter-claims. The simple and irrefutable Palestinian demand for international condemnation of political movements and militarized societies which oppressed the women and children of weaker Third World communities was declared an anti-feminist cause. United States delegates seriously attempted to banish all political arguments from these conferences in a thinly-disguised effort aimed at protecting Israel's international image.[1] The UN document which emerged from the Nairobi deliberations, nevertheless, did call on all nations to safeguard the rights of women and children in time of war. It specifically mentioned Palestinian victims of this type of oppression.

Beginning in December of 1987, the Intifida inaugurated a new phase of the Palestinian national struggle in the West Bank and Gaza. More than ever before, Palestinian women became important actors in the civil disobedience campaign engulfing the occupied territories. The women's involvement, often in direct and open defiance of the Israeli occupation authorities as demonstrators and stone throwers, has finally activated all sectors of the female population. It has been suggested that political and agitational roles assumed by Palestinian women were really a conservative gesture in defense of a conservative institution, namely the family. In reality, women have always been active in defense of society at large. The intensification of Israeli political and economic oppression since 1967 has pervaded all Palestinian institutions, even the family. The Israelis, however, have never spared the women any punishment, however harsh. Lately, recognizing the important role of women in the Intifada, the Israelis have retaliated against them by closing many of their welfare institutions and illegalizing their work committees. This is a concerted attack on a very effective segment of the Palestinian population and a demonstration of the occupation's insidious effects on women and children.

What kind of feminists are these Palestinians? Efforts by Israeli women to reach them through feminist rhetoric have failed. Only Israeli women organized against the Israeli invasion of Lebanon or opposed to the militaristic and chauvinist aspects of Israeli society have succeeded in linking up with Palestinian women.[2] The linkage, however, has been

---

[1]Ellen Cantarow, "Zionism, Anti-Semitism and Jewish Identity in the Women's Movement," Middle East Report, vol. 18, no. 154 (Sept.-Oct., 1988), pp. 38-43.

[2]"Women in Black," Al-Fajr (April 3, 1988), p. 9.

erratic, since the Palestinians' goals at this stage of the national struggle revolve around purely nationalist goals such as survival and independence. Most Israeli women appear to be unable or unwilling to adopt these as their goals. Palestinian women have always chosen political and national goals over limited legal and economic objectives. They often remind us that until the creation of a state of their own, their enemy will remain Israel militarism and not Palestinian males. It is this strong sense of national identity which has catapulted Palestinian women to the front lines of the Intifida's battles.

MODERN PALESTINIAN LITERATURE

Issa J. Boullata

As in other regions of the Arab world, poetry in Palestine was the most important literary genre when the 20th century opened. Couched in a traditional style, its themes revolved around a limited array of subjects in imitation of old classical poets, but with little innovation and imagination. After the institution of the Ottoman constitution in 1908,* Palestinian journalism began to introduce new ideas of freedom, and also greater openness to the outside world. It developed a modern prose that gradually emancipated itself from the verbal and rhyme embellishments characteristic of Arabic prose in the previous several centuries of literary decadence. This gave poetry an impetus to venture and concern itself with new themes and styles as Palestinian society was growing and entering the modern world.

Poets began to show increasing interest in social and political matters. They expressed fears that their cultural identity and national integrity were threatened by the Zionist movement. Poets like Is'af al-Nashashibi (1882-1948) and Wadi' al-Bustani (1888-1954), using classical styles, spoke out to alert the Palestinians. After the Balfour Declaration of 1917 promised a homeland in Palestine for the Jews, and after the British Mandate was imposed in 1922 on the Palestinian people in order to implement it, this threat became a dominant theme in Palestinian poetry, as in Palestinian life in general. Poets like Iskandar al-Khuri al-Baytajali (1890-1978) and Abu Salma (1909-1980) gave it a lot of attention in their poems.

But it was Ibrahim Tuqan (1905-1941) who was to become the leading poet of Palestine under the British Mandate, not only because he treated this theme most forcefully and eloquently, but also because of his new poetic techniques and innovative imagination when expressing it and when dealing with other themes. His poetic creativity was consonant with developments in Arabic poetry in other parts of the Arab world. Tuqan's poetry denounced Zionism and British collusion, condemned traitors and land brokers, extolled Palestinian heroes and martyrs, and found fit also to celebrate the joys of life and love, human aspirations

---

*On July 24, 1908, Sultan Abd al-Hamid agreed to the ultimatum of the Society of Union and Progress for the restoral of the "Midhat" constitution of 1878, and to the calling of elections for the second Turkish parliament.

72

often marred by colonial injustices in Palestine. Following in his footsteps, 'Abd al-Rahim Mahmud (1913-1948) defended the Palestinian cause in his poetry and died in the battle of al-Shajara in the 1948 war.

As the British Mandate ended in 1948 and Israel was established, the Palestinian poets found themselves dispersed with their people. Some were in refugee camps, having been deprived of their lands and their homes; others were in exile outside Palestine, ever yearning to return to their homeland; others still were under Israeli control within the boundaries of the new state, never treated as full citizens. Wherever they were, the love of their homeland continued naturally to be a major theme of their poetry.

Mahmud Darwish (b. 1942), who lived in Israel until 1971, then in Lebanon until chased out by the Israeli invasion of 1982, expresses his love of Palestine -- whether he resides in Paris, Nicosia, Tunis, or anywhere in the world -- in terms of eternal attachment to the soil of his homeland, often symbolized as a human sweetheart. His daring poetic techniques in free verse and his vivid and unfettered imagination permit him to use the Arabic language in an unprecedented, creative way that fuses memories of his Palestinian paradise with hopes of human dignity and peace in it, for both its people and their enemies. As he celebrates the great indomitable qualities of the human spirit and calls for respect for human values, he remains the most important Palestinian poet now alive. The colleagues of his youth, Samih al-Qasim (b. 1939), Tawfiq Zayyad (b. 1932), and Salim Jubran (b. 1941) continue in Israel to give hope to Palestinians through their poetry.

The other parts of Palestine, held temporarily by Jordan and Egypt since 1948 (the 'West Bank' and the 'Gaza Strip' respectively), then occupied by Israel since 1967, produced similar poets whose aspirations for freedom and self-determination dominated their poetic themes. Fadwa Tuqan (b. 1917) abandoned her earlier love topics to embrace those relating to her people's drive for justice and independence. She still lives in her native Nablus. Harun Hashim Rashid (b. 1930) left his native Gaza and continues to write today of his personal and national tragedy in Tunis as he did when in his homeland under Israeli occupation.

Palestinians living in exile outside their original homeland include several well-known poets. Among them Tawfiq Sayigh (1923-1971) and Jabra Ibrahim Jabra (b. 1919) have written prose poems of rare beauty, remembering their youth in the homeland. While Sayigh cries out to God in his suffering from a love mangled by a heedless world, Jabra criticizes the inept Arab ways of regaining the homeland. Kamal Nasir (1925-1973) sang of a joyous return in exquisite verse till he was gunned down by Israelis at his home in Beirut. Rashid Husayn (1936-1977) and Fawzi al-Asmar (b. 1937), Israeli citizens often imprisoned for their ideas at home, had to leave Israel for the United States in order to continue their struggle in a free world. Husayn, who had translated poems by Hayyim Bialik from Hebrew into Arabic, died in a fire at his New York apartment; al-Asmar lives in Washington, D.C.; his Hebrew autobiography, To Be an Arab in Israel, sums up the Palestinian ordeal, and has been translated into English, Arabic, and other languages.

Meanwhile, younger Palestinian poets everywhere, under occupation and in exile, continue to sing of the day of national salvation and liberation. The Intifada (uprising) that started on December 9, 1987, against Israeli occupation, has given all Palestinians further hope and fired the imagination of their poets in an indelible, new way.

Palestinian literature in prose had a development parallel to that in verse. Early in the 20th century, it rid itself of traditional embellishments and verbal conceits common in the preceding period of literary decadence and, through journalism, acquired a sprightly and practical character. The main literary genre in prose was the essay, and its acknowledged masters were Is'af al-Nashashibi (1881-1948) and Khalil al-Sakakini (1878-1953). The former retained vestiges of the traditional style emphasizing verbal virtuosity; the latter carved for himself a personal style undaunted by tradition. Younger writers were influenced by al-Sakakini as, like him, they dealt with social, political, literary, and general cultural topics in their essays.

The flexibility of literary prose soon lent itself to the writing of fiction. Khalil Baydas (1875-1949) was a pioneer both in his stories and his translations, and was instrumental in popularizing the art of fiction through his monthly al-Nafa'is al-'Asriyya.

Fiction became a respectable art by the end of the Second World War and included such votaries as Najati Sidqi (b. 1905) and Mahmud Sayf al-Din al-Irani (1914-1978), who enriched Palestinian literature with their translations and their short stories. A younger contemporary, Samira 'Azzam (1927-1967), became noted, like them, for her short stories dealing with social issues related to the oppressed in society, but she had deeper insight into the character of women and other individuals in difficulties.

As fiction began to vie with poetry by the time the Palestine tragedy of 1948 occurred, it was increasingly used thereafter to portray the disrupted life of Palestinians. Ghassan Kanafani (1936-1972) was one of the earliest to depict life in the Palestinian refugee camps, being himself a refugee, initially in Damascus. Submissiveness, frustration, rebelliousness, resilience, indignation, and the taking up of arms are all compellingly evident as attitudes of Palestinian characters in his fiction. While his novel, Men in the Sun (1963), tells the story of three refugees who die silently in the empty water tank of a truck in their attempt to be smuggled into Kuwait to find work and individual salvation, his later novel, Return to Haifa (1968), portrays a character who realizes that armed struggle alone can achieve true individual and national salvation. Kanafani was killed with his niece in Beirut by Israeli agents when his booby-trapped car blew up as he started it.

Jabra Ibrahim Jabra (b. 1919), who now lives in Baghdad, has written several short stories and novels. His novel, The Ship (1970), tells the story of the Arab passengers on a ship cruising the Mediterranean, among whom the Palestinian alone has a strong attachment to his homeland, while the others, representing decadent bourgeois Arabs, remain desperately lost in their attempt to escape from conditions in their home countries. In Jabra's novel, The Search for Walid Mas'ud, a similarly rich Palestinian who has achieved success away from his homeland, disappears mysteriously and the search for him leads the reader to believe he has joined the PLO freedom-fighters.

Emile Habibi (b. 1921), an Israeli Arab and former Knesset member, conveys through the short stories in his Sextet of the Six Days (1969) the sense of Palestinian unity when, after the Six-Day War of 1967, Israeli Arabs meet other Palestinians from whom they had been separated for about twenty years. In his novel, The Mysterious Events Leading to the Disappearance of Sa'id, the Ill-fated Pess-optimist, Habibi portrays in a masterful satirical style the feelings of an Israeli Arab who, despite his loyalty to Israel, continues to live in constant anxiety while awaiting a solution to the Palestine problem.

Another Israeli Arab, Anton Shammas (b. 1950), has written an autobiographical novel in Hebrew entitled Arabesques (1986), which has been hailed as a modern masterpiece of the Hebrew language. Now also available in English and French (1988), it affirms the social and emotional power of the deep roots that Palestinians have in their homeland. It tells the story of generations of the narrator's family in the Palestinian village of Fassuta in Upper Galilee, from the 12th century invasion of the Crusades to the 1982 massacre of Palestinians at Sabra and Shatila in Lebanon. It ends with a fitting climax when finally the Israeli Arab narrator meets with his cousin and namesake, from whom he had been long separated because he had been lost as a baby in Beirut and is now a researcher at the Centre of Palestine Studies there.

Sahar Khalifah (b. 1941), who teaches at Bir Zeit University in Palestine, has written several novels, the first of which was confiscated by Israeli authorities. One of her later novels, Wild Thorns (1976), has been translated into Hebrew, English and French. It tells the story of a young Palestinian who returns to occupied Palestine from the Persian Gulf and undertakes a sabotage mission in order to stop buses from transporting Palestinian workers into Israel as cheap labor. The novel captures the dilemmas of Palestinians under Israeli occupation, determined to survive and gain independence but realizing the limitations of their determination if not supported by Arab and international will for a decisive solution.

Though Yahya Yakhlif (b. 1945) sets the action of one of his novels, Najran below Zero (1975), in Arabia, where in the 1960's the Yemeni royalists were finally defeated, he deals in reality with poverty and political coercion in Arab society. He suggests the necessity of revolutionary change in the Arab world, if Palestinians and other Arabs are ever to enjoy the gifts of peace, justice and prosperity.

If Palestinian literature is dominated by themes of national destiny and liberation, it must be remembered that the Palestinians are a nation threatened with extinction. They are daily decimated, ill-treated, coerced, and repressed under the eyes of the civilized world; they are often subjected to massacres, air raids, destruction of their homes, confiscation of their land and property, and attempts to eliminate them and liquidate their culture; they are maligned and reviled, their history is perverted and disfigured, and all truth about them is distorted by their powerful enemies with powerful allies. Their human and civil rights are conspicuously violated with little objection or intervention by western society, and their homeland continues to be occupied by military force. No wonder they have to depend on themselves to preserve their identity, their integrity as a people, and their very life. Their poets, novelists, essayists, short story writers and other intellectuals are only doing their duty to shore up the human spirit in those still alive, despite unspeakable tragedies. They hope for better days to come when they can at last live in peace with their former enemies, as the latter and the virtually silent world at large become increasingly humanized by art, if not by other means.

76

THE PALESTINE LIBERATION ORGANIZATION (PLO)

(Adapted from A Profile of the Palestinian People, by Edward W. Said, et. al.)

In the world today there are almost five million Palestinians -- those born in Palestine and their offspring born there or in areas after dispersion. Nowhere do these people enjoy or exercise any political rights as Palestinians; yet they are determined on attaining a normal political status. They are committed to a struggle for national self-determination, including the right to independence and sovereignty in their homeland, the right of return, and the right of national identity.

Between 1948 and 1967, Palestine ceased to exist as a political and administrative entity. As a people, the Palestinians were dispersed and fragmented. They had no real authority to guide, direct and sustain their national life. They had no control over their cultural, social and economic institutions. They faced active discrimination everywhere: abject social and economic conditions within Israel and in exile. But despite these difficulties, Palestinians have continued to engage in political activity motivated by two broad imperatives: first, to continue the struggle to achieve their national rights; second, to direct existing political opportunities toward improving their social, economic and educational conditions.

In the early years, following the dismemberment of their country, Palestinians strove to forge an authority capable of addressing itself to the issues of the inherent national rights of their people. These early attempts at political organization were subjected to routine control and manipulation by "host" Arab country political ambitions and goals. It was not until 1964 that the Palestine National Congress, at its meeting in Jerusalem, resolved to establish the Palestine Liberation Organization and gave it a mandate to mobilize the Palestinian people for the task of liberating Palestine.

For about three years after its emergence, the PLO struggled to define itself and to press its program on its dispersed Palestinian constituency, on the Arab region, and on the world. In those years the challenge to its legitimacy came essentially from three different sources. Not surprisingly, it came from Israel, which saw in it the reincarnation of the old Palestinian people it thought had vanished. It came from Jordan, too, which perceived it as a threat to its political system and a challenge to its incorporation of the West Bank into the Jordanian state, should the

Palestinians there identify too closely with the PLO. The third challenge to the PLO came from Palestinian militants, who had been organized underground for national liberation, and who viewed the organization and its leaders as instruments of the Pan-Arab politics of Egypt and neither sufficiently militant nor independent in decision-making.

From a very turbulent beginning, the PLO in due course acquired legitimacy from the consensus of the Palestinian people. At the Rabat Summit Conference in 1974 the Arab States recognized the PLO as the legitimate representative of the Palestinian people. The PLO eventually obtained similar recognition from 132 countries. In the same year, the General Assembly passed a resolution inviting the PLO to participate in the United Nations as an observer, and it acquired parallel status in all specialized agencies of the UN. At present, the PLO maintains diplomatic-informational missions in all UN agencies and in the capitals of some ninety countries, including Canada. The Palestine Information Office in Ottawa serves to provide Canadians with updated information on events in the Middle East.

Today, the PLO represents a kind of embryonic Palestinian state and government. Its constituency is the entirety of the Palestinian people. Over the years the Palestinians, no matter how subjugated or displaced, have retained a distinct and durable consciousness of themselves as a national community; in response the PLO has developed a structure designed to address the needs and the aspirations of its constituency. Recent Israeli and non-Israeli public opinion polls have show that almost 98 percent of the Palestinians in the West Bank favour the establishment of an independent Palestinian state; well over 85 percent would like the PLO to head such a state. A poll conducted in the Gaza Strip in 1983 reveals that 86.4 percent view the PLO as a legitimate representative of the Palestinian people and 81.3 percent viewed the PLO as the sole legitimate representative. A 1986 poll conducted in Gaza and on the West Bank showed that 93.5 percent viewed the PLO as the sole legitimate representative of the Palestinian people.

The Palestinian National Council (PNC) is the highest policy-making body of the Palestine Liberation Organization. At present, the Council is composed of 394 members presumed to represent all sectors of the Palestinian people, geographically and culturally. (The Council has allocated certain seats to Palestinians in the occupied areas, but Israeli control has prevented those members from attending the sessions of the Council.) The membership of the Council is drawn from three separate categories: the militant organizations (Fatah, Popular Front for the Liberation of Palestine, Popular Democratic Front, etc.) in proportion to their actual or presumed strength; popular associations such as teachers' unions, women's, students', writers' or workers' unions; and independents (see chart). Function, geography and politics play important roles in the designation of the membership in the Council. The Council, as the representative of the Palestinian people, symbolizes Palestinian pluralism; it is a multi-party council and is intended to reflect all political tendencies present in the Palestinian political community.

The Council debates issues of concern to Palestinians at its meetings scheduled at intervals of 2-3 years because of the dispersal of the Palestinian people. Usually these meetings last about one week, at the end of which two sets of action are adopted. One deals with the policies that the executive is to pursue in the coming period, policies relating to such matters as finance, military activities, political strategy, or bureaucratic functions, such as the creation of various departments -- education, social welfare, culture, etc. The second action of the Council is the election of the Executive Committee and its chairman. Thus far the practice has been to elect by secret ballot fifteen persons who for all practical purposes act as the Palestinian cabinet. The Executive Committee is responsible for implementing the policies the Council had adopted. The committee elects its chairman. Mr. Yasir Arafat has filled this post since 1969. Essentially the chairman assumes the function of president and prime minister; each member of the Executive Committee is responsible for a particular functional department. These departments are charged with advancing the social, economic, cultural, educational and military interests of the Palestinian people. Over the years, they have fostered the development of a distinct Palestinian Bureaucracy subject to rules and regulations approved by the Palestine National Council. Excluding the military cadres, the PLO civil service now numbers some eight thousand persons. The Council has also created additional governmental authorities. It has established higher councils for education, for culture, for literacy, for economic development, a Palestine National Fund (combining treasury and commerce), and a Palestine Red Crescent Society (public health, including hospitals and clinics).

These structures supply a network of Palestinian national institutions for the benefit of Palestinians everywhere. Through them, the PLO can assist the dispersed Palestinian communities in obtaining jobs, in placing students at institutions of higher learning in the host societies, in manning educational establishments, in enhancing Palestinian cultural and economic growth. The most striking success of this institutional growth and development took place in Lebanon, where the estimated four hundred thousand Palestinians began to form an embryonic Palestinian society free from the constraints of either Israeli occupation or total control by a host government. It was in Lebanon that a good proportion of the Palestinian bureaucracy was to be found; it was in Lebanon that Palestinian cultural, economic and social institutions were to develop; and it was in Lebanon that the Palestinian identity began really to re-coalesce. All this was accomplished with considerable difficulty and without the full cooperation of the Lebanese government. But the healthy development of the Palestinian community in Lebanon made it inevitable that Israel should see it as a challenge, and attempt its destruction.

On June 4, 1982, Israel carried out massive air raids against Palestinian areas in Beirut; it continued these raids on Beirut and the entirety of south Lebanon on the fifth of June. On the sixth, its army, an estimated one hundred thousand men backed by the air force and navy, marched on Lebanon with the public objective of obtaining "Peace for Galilee". Israel later admitted that its objective was to destroy the PLO and its infrastructure in Lebanon.

In the course of two and one half months Israel's vastly destructive campaign took the lives of as many as forty thousand Palestinians and Lebanese, seriously injured over one hundred thousand persons and left over one-half million homeless. Israel succeeded in destroying the major part of Palestinian political and social institutions in Lebanon. The entire Palestinian health program and facilities were destroyed; economic enterprises (SAMED, for example) were wiped out; communication systems -- radio, newspapers, and publishing houses -- were either looted or destroyed. Palestinian settlements in Lebanon from Rashidiyya in the south to the Fakhani district of West Beirut were reduced to rubble. The only Palestinian community to have raised itself form the wreckage of Palestine in 1948, and to have achieved a condition of relative autonomy, was willfully destroyed. Thousands of Palestinians were expelled from Lebanon and those that remained have endured enormous political, economic, and social hardships, and continue to do so.

As a result of Israel's assault on Lebanon and the Palestinians residing there, the overall Palestinian situation has become considerably more complex. Not only is the Palestinian liberation effort temporarily frustrated, but the goal of independence for the West Bank and Gaza -- something that would ameliorate the Palestinian plight significantly and that is fully supported by international consensus as expressed by the United Nations -- seems to be less realizable. The Palestinian hope for return to Palestine, as mandated by the United Nations, has grown much dimmer with the daily influx of those expelled from both occupied Palestine and occupied Lebanon who drift into neighboring countries such as Syria and Jordan. Without question, the loss of the Lebanese offices and land base has complicated PLO operations and reduced its ability to enhance the welfare and security of the Palestinian people.

The Palestine National Charter adopted in 1964 by the Palestine National Congress outlined the general principles and ideas that should guide Palestinian action. It also delineated, although with considerable ambiguity, the path to the realization of the formulated goal of the liberation of Palestine (which then meant only pre-1967, post-1948 Israel). The National Council of 1968 and its later amplifications projected a solution to the question of Palestine consistent not only with Palestinian self-determination but also with the reality of an Israeli Jewish presence in Palestine-Israel. The projected solution dealt forthrightly with the anomalous status of both the West Bank and Gaza. The highly organized militant groups of the PLO proposed a vision of a democratic secular polity for Palestine, in which sectarian or national influences would play no part. Both Zionism and Arab nationalism were thus rejected as a basis for the future Palestinian state. Underlying that vision was the awareness of the existence of two peoples on the same land, one Palestinian Arab -- the other Israeli Jewish. The national affiliation of Palestinians with the Arab people was of no consequence to the political organization of the projected Palestine; similarly the religious affiliation of Israelis with Jews elsewhere was to entail no special political right or obligation. The vision of the democratic secular polity was not of one consisting of two separate and hostile communities, but of persons whose individual rights were primary and equal. This concept challenged both Israeli Jews and Palestinian Arabs to accept coexistence in the same polity on the basis of full equality.

It was fully realized that this goal conflicted with Zionism and its embodiment in Israel. Additionally, the movement viewed Israel as an extension of European-American imperialism which therefore would marshal its resources to resist the new formulation. Achievement of the first principle -- the establishment of a democratic secular polity in Palestine -- could not be realized except by adherence to a second principle -- the necessity for armed struggle by the Palestinian masses. Towards that end, the PLO undertook to mobilize and organize the Palestinians, and it subsequently recruited militant cadres and obtained material and political support for that program. As it did so, the PLO succeeded in organizing and in focusing the loyalty of the Palestinian people, as well as in challenging the legitimacy of the Arab states' exercise of control over Palestinians within their domain. The PLO additionally understood that Israel's control of the West Bank and Gaza must be challenged by all means, including militant action, and it therefore rendered material, political, and economic support to Palestinians there to resist Israel's occupation. Finally, as representative of the Palestinian people everywhere, the PLO viewed its functions as including its duty to organize the Palestinian communities everywhere and to provide them with support, security and welfare.

The political platform of the PLO has changed over the past two decades. For example, the modification of the Palestinian program aiming at the creation of a democratic secular state in all of Palestine took place within the Palestine National Council, which adopted a Provisional Program that accepted de facto Palestinian authority over the West Bank and Gaza should Israel withdraw; this was subsequently amended in 1977 to demand an independent Palestinian state under the control of the Palestine Liberation Organization. It was in the pursuit of that modified program that the Executive Committee made its appeal in the United Nations in 1981 to support the establishment of an independent Palestinian state specifically in the West Bank and Gaza. Since 1983, the PLO has repeatedly called for the convening of an international peace conference under the auspices of the United Nations. The PLO has accepted Security Council resolutions 242 and 338, within the context of all relevant United Nations resolutions.

On November 15, 1988, the Palestine National Council declared the State of Palestine, basing its status in international law on UN Resolution 181 (see Documents) which partitioned Palestine into a Jewish and an Arab Palestinian state. The PNC thereby formally accepted a two-state solution. A month later following his address to the UN General Assembly convened in Geneva to hear him, Chairman Arafat explicitly accepted Resolutions 242 and 338, renounced terrorism in all its forms and accepted the right of all states in the area to live in peace, including Palestine and Israel. Within hours, the U.S. announced that it was prepared to embark upon "substantive dialogue" with PLO representatives. The talks which followed were the first since 1974 when then Secretary of State, Henry Kissenger imposed a ban on any direct U.S.-PLO contacts until the PLO recognized Israel's right to exist, accepted Security Council Resolutions 242 and 338 and renounced terrorism.

As the PLO reorganizes and maps out its alternative strategies to carry on its mandate, it does so fully confident of the backing of a Palestinian national consensus. No matter the jurisdiction exercised over them, no matter the conditions under which they suffer, the 5.8 million Palestinians continue to press for return to an independent Palestinian

State. In that effort they have the growing support of the world community.

STRUCTURE OF THE PLO

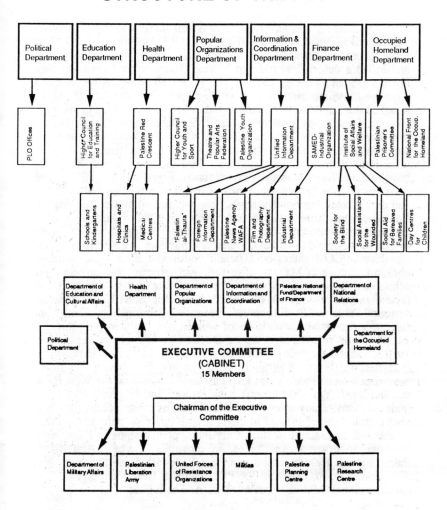

TERRORISTS OR FREEDOM FIGHTERS?
SOLDIERS OR SAVAGES?

James A. Graff

Are PLO fighters terrorists? Are Israeli soldiers savages? Haven't PLO guerillas hijacked or blown up passenger planes in the early '70's, taken Israeli athletes hostage at Munich, and even hijacked a cruise ship and killed a defenseless old man? Yes. But haven't Israeli jets shot down a Libyan passenger plane (1972) killing all on board, bombed and destroyed civilian aircraft at Beirut airport? Haven't Israeli sailors hijacked ships and taken Palestinian and Lebanese passengers to prison in Israel? Haven't they even sunk ships and machine-gunned survivors in the water? Yes. But haven't PLO fighters planted bombs in supermarkets, on roads, on buses in Israel, and fired rockets at (admittedly armed) "settlements" near the Lebanese border? Yes. But haven't Israeli jets bombed Palestinian refugee camps, killing and maiming thousands upon thousands of Palestinian women and children, and didn't Israeli jets bomb schools, hospitals and apartment buildings in Lebanon when Israel invaded that country in 1982? Didn't they drop fragmentation bombs, using "cluster bombs" whose bomblets were especially designed to attract children and blow up in their hands? Yes. But didn't PLO fighters hold Israeli youth and even some younger children hostage at Ma' Lot after they were discovered, seizing their school and those inside to bargain for the release of their comrades and their own safe passage out of Israel? Yes. But didn't Israeli generals surround Sabra and Shatilla camps, preventing Palestinian civilians from fleeing and watching truckloads of women and children pass through their lines to be butchered during the massacres there in September, 1982? And did they not permit their client Lebanese militia to massacre Palestinian civilians of all ages near Sidon and Tyre which they held? Yes. But haven't Palestinians killed Israeli "settlers" on the West Bank and in Gaza? Yes. But haven't Israeli troops and "settlers" killed and maimed many, many more Palestinian civilians there, beaten them up, even tortured them? Yes. But didn't Jewish terrorists before Israel was established massacre Palestinian civilians, plant bombs in Palestinian markets, in cinemas, on buses, in mosques ... yes. And didn't Palestinians in Hebron massacre almost 20 Jewish families? Yes. But didn't Israeli troops massacre 300 Palestinians at Dawainah in 1948, first clubbing all the children to death? Yes. And so it goes.

About 20 Israeli civilians are killed each year in Palestinian attacks on clearly civilian targets. Ordinary murder accounts for 40-60 victims, suicide for 200, and traffic accidents for an average of 425. Between 1978 and 1982, attacks on Jewish settlements in northern Israel (Galilee) killed 29. Despite an 11-month cease-fire, Israel gave as its official reason for invading Lebanon in 1982 that it was necessary to put an end, once and for all, to PLO attacks on those settlements.* Over a six-year period from 1982 to December 9, 1987, 134 Palestinian civilians in the Occupied Territories have been killed, some by "settlers", most by Israeli soldiers using live ammunition to put down demonstrations. From 1983 to 1987, however, the death toll among Palestinian civilians due to Israeli air attacks and shellings have been in the thousands. Early in September 1987, a bombing attack on a camp near Sidon killed over 55 people, all civilians, mostly women and children. From June 5 until early September 1982, over 30,000 Palestinian and Lebanese civilians were killed and over 100,000 wounded by Israeli bombing and shelling of population centres in a war with the highest civilian casualty percentage toll in history -- 92 percent of all casualities were civilians.

Does it matter whether the people who target civilians wear uniforms? Does it matter whether they are soldiers in a regular army or guerilla fighters? Well, regular armies can kill and maim many more and do because they have the firepower, the planes, the bombs and the naval power. But does that make soldiers targetting civilians acceptable and guerillas targetting civilians somehow wrong? Surely, it is immoral to attack civilians whether on a large or small scale. If guerilla fighters should be called "terrorists" when they attack innocent civilians, so should soldiers and governments when they, too, attack innocent civilians. Although warfare itself is, by its nature, an evil because it is the killing, maiming, widowing, and orphaning of people, the destruction of their homes and cherished possessions, and the shattering of many lives, it is morally imperative to confine and contain those evils once war has broken out. Governments can use terror and do so on a much larger scale than guerilla organizations.

Suppose someone called Israeli soldiers "savages" because of their brutal beatings and killings witnessed on North American TV screens during the Revolt of the Youth in the Occupied Territories, he would be morally condemning those soldiers for their behaviour. Now suppose someone said that Israel used state terror in Lebanon and in the Occupied Territories, and was a "terrorist state", he would also be condemning

---

* David Shipler, <u>Arab and Jew: Wounded Spirits in a Promised Land</u>, p. 84.

Israel morally for its behaviour. He would have to support the charge by describing, as we have done above, its targetting civilians and the scale and nature of the violence it used against them. If someone called a Palestinian guerilla attack a "terrorist attack", he would be morally condemning the attack and would also have to defend his charge by showing that innocent civilians were attacked or by describing the nature and scale of the violence used. In both cases, 'terrorist' and 'terrorism' would be used to condemn, and, in each case, the same kinds of facts would have to be cited to support the charge. 'Terrorists', like 'savages', is a term used to condemn people for what they have done. If we say that a government uses terror to control a population or in fighting a war, we are condemning that government's policies as immoral because they involve the use of tactics designed to terrorize a civilian population. Those tactics have to involve attacks and threats of attacks on civilians, the use of terrible violence against them or even against guerilla fighters who have their support, and who are trying either to liberate their country or to overthrow its oppressive regime. If we call a guerilla organization a "terrorist organization", we imply that the organization has a clear policy of attacking civilian targets, or of using terrible violence against enemy soldiers or civilians to terrorize their enemy. What is terror for the goose (guerillas, say), is terror for the gander (governments).

Many governments want to label groups fighting them as "terrorists" as a way of making themselves look decent when they do similar or worse things to their enemies. The Nazis labelled all the resistance fighters trying to free their countries from Nazi occupation in World War II (1939-45), "terrorists", while terrorizing their conquered subjects. It is important to distinguish, then, between legitimate armed resistance to oppression and to a conqueror on the one hand, and terrorism on the other. In Europe, resistance movements did use terror, especially against the families of Nazi collaborators and informers and against those they feared might collaborate. The justice of their cause did not make those tactics right, but those tactics did not make the Nazi cause somehow more decent either. One of the real moral issues underlying accusations of terrorism, is the nature and scope of violence which has to count as an acceptable evil in armed conflict. The other central moral issue has to do with setting the limits to morally acceptable targets in armed conflict. Those issues get buried when people accept, without argument, either that Israel is a terrorist state or that the PLO is a terrorist organization. The truth seems to be that Israel has used large-scale terror in controlling Palestinians under occupation and against Palestinian civilians in Lebanon. It is also true that the PLO has used small-scale terror against Israelis in Israel and abroad. Both, however, also attack acceptable, i.e., clearly military targets, and each has ended up killing civilians by mistake. Both have political objectives in using terror. The Israelis want to weaken, if not destroy, the PLO because it does represent the aspirations of the Palestinians for a state of their own in the Occupied Territories and could not only speak for them, but operate such a state. They want to ensure that there is no effective Palestinian political organization in those Territories, and no effective Palestinian military or political movement outside, PLO or otherwise. If these objectives change, peace may be possible. For its part, the PLO wants to maintain a sense of insecurity among Israelis and to show that it leads the resistance to Israel's occupation of Palestinian lands and to keep up pressure which may eventually bring the overwhelmingly more powerful Israeli government to negotiate a settlement.

In any war, innocents are killed and maimed. Disrupting enemy communications, transportation systems, government services, arms industry, economic life are all elements of conventional and guerilla warfare. The line between terrorism and legitimate targetting, with the loss of civilian life and damage to civilian property, is not always easy to draw and is particularly more difficult to draw in a guerilla war. Soldiers cannot easily tell a guerilla from a civilian and cannot always easily distinguish civilian from military targets. Guerillas cannot themselves always easily distinguish armed settlements from para-military installations, or draw a clear line between an economic target and a clearly off-limits civilian target. There are large grey areas, but that does not mean that there are no clear-cut cases of state terror on the one hand, or subnational terror on the other.

Both sides have condemned acts of terrorism and denied accusations levelled against them. The PLO has condemned "acts of terrorism whether by individuals or states, including acts of terrorism committed by Israel against the Palestinian people and the Arab nation." Israel has long branded the PLO as a "terrorist organization" and labels any PLO attack, whether on a military or civilian target, a "terrorist attack." It has condemned "international terrorism" and defended its terror as "counter-terror," "retaliation," "pre-emptive attack," or "suppressing Arab violence," "restoring law and order," or "self-defense." The rhetoric, while serving propaganda purposes, tends to prolong the by now 40 year-old Palestinian-Israeli war. It tends, too, to "justify" the very real, large-scale sufferings of Palestinians, on the one hand, and to inflame the desire for revenge on both sides.

What is terrorism then? We can characterize terrorism by saying that it involves the threat of the use of violence for broadly political objectives; either the targets of violence are morally illegitimate targets, or the scale or nature of the violence used or threatened is morally illegitimate. Since people who play no role or who are unable to play an active role in some conflict have clearly in no way contributed directly to the shedding of blood, they are innocent and should not be targetted. They are the bystanders and the innocent civilians whose targetting is one major reason for labelling an attack, a "terrorist act." When the unarmed, the disarmed, the sick, and the wounded are deliberately attacked, no one can feel safe. When children and youths are brutally beaten, prisoners tortured, homes shot at or bombed, no one can feel safe. When brutality, maiming weapons and weapons of mass slaughter are used, and when ordinary civilians, children, the aged, the wounded and sick are targetted, the target population is terrorized. In a political context, choices of such methods of violence and of such targets is terrorism.

Terrorism was a major instrument in the creation of the State of Israel and in clearing Jewish-held areas of their Palestinian populations. It was used in establishing many other states, including the U.S., and it has always generated terror as a response, whether initiated by governing authorities or by organizations fighting them. Although it is very important to urge parties to a violent conflict to use restraint and care in their choice of targets, weapons and methods of treating the "enemies" within their control, it is also important to urge them to negotiate a just and compassionate political settlement so that the violence and suffering on both sides can be brought to an end.

Are PLO guerillas freedom fighters or terrorists? Well, some have committed acts of terrorism. In 1985, however, the PLO had arranged to try four guerillas who had hijacked the cruise ship, Achille Lauro, but the Americans forced the Egyptian plane carrying them from Cairo to Tunis to land at an American base in Italy and finally released the four to Italian police after an armed confrontation. Are Israeli soldiers savages? Well, some have behaved savagely. But some Israeli officers and ordinary soldiers refused to fire on children and women in Lebanon, others refused to serve there, and some have refused to serve in the Occupied Territories and demonstrated against their government's "Iron Fist" policies there. Is Israel a terrorist state? It has used state terror. Is the PLO a terrorist organization? The various guerilla organizations which make up its military wing have used terror. It is also true that Israel has attacked "legitimate" military targets and so has the PLO. What matters is that the massive violence Israel uses against Palestinians and the small-scale violence Palestinians use against Israel be brought to an end. That is what matters most, and not whether one or both of the contenders is more deserving of the label, "terrorist".

CANADA, ISRAEL AND THE PALESTINIANS

Peyton Lyon, James A. Graff and Farid Ohan

Canada is not now a major actor in the politics of the Middle East. It was not always so, and need not be so in the future. Two Canadians, Justice Ivan Rand of the Supreme Court, and Lester B. Pearson, then a senior Canadian diplomat, played key roles in 1947 in the creation and recognition of the new state of Israel. Nine years later, Pearson, having become Canadian foreign minister, earned the Nobel Peace Prize for leading in the establishment of the first United Nations peace-keeping force (UNEF). UNEF defused for a time the crisis in the Suez region caused by an invasion of Egypt by Israel, France and Britain. UNEF's first commander was another great Canadian, Lt. General E.L.M. Burns. Canadian troops, representing 1.6 percent of Canada's armed forces, are still serving on three peace-keeping forces in the immediate vicinity of Israel.

Canada now has ten embassies spread among fifteen countries of the Middle East. These embassies display an acute interest in the continuing strife between Israel and its Arab neighbours.

Despite its past record, and current military and diplomatic presence, Canada now exerts almost no influence in the Middle East peace process. Its spokesmen have acknowledged that, if we stumble into the third and final world war, the likeliest flash point for its start is the Middle East. Only here do we find the coincidence of unsatisfied territorial claims, a serious sense of injustice, vital energy resources, and competing super-power interests. Our diplomatic presence, however, is largely devoted to trade. This trade is important for its quality, even though it accounts for only about 1 percent of Canada's total trade. Trade and the sale of Canadian services to the Arab World together represent roughly $4.5 billion yearly.

Canada usually has not sought to influence the Middle East policies of our major ally, the United States, whose annual subsidies to Israel run into billions. These subsidies are essential to the maintenance of the Israeli military establishment, by far the strongest in the Middle East. Only the United States is now in a position effectively to press Israel to implement the United Nations' resolutions that would end its heavy-handed military occupation of Gaza, the West Bank and the Golan Heights. The Golan Heights are a part of Syria conquered by Israel in 1967 and later formally annexed in violation of international law.

Canada's position is not identical to that of the United States. Washington has given almost automatic backing to Israel and has used its veto in the Security Council time after time to prevent substantive action. Canada is often critical of Israeli actions. An astonishing exception was Prime Minister Mulroney's statement of December 21, 1987, condoning the Israeli use of force to suppress demonstrations in Gaza and the West Bank, and denying that Israel violates human rights. By December 21, 19 Palestinians had been shot to death and over 200 seriously wounded by Israeli gunfire. Hundreds had been savagely beaten by Israeli troops and hundreds more detained. Their troops had tear-gassed Gaza's al-Shifa Hospital, forcing their way in, beating medical personnel and smashing equipment. Later on, Canada did express concern at Israel's excessive use of force.

Unlike the U.S., Canada would accept independent statehood for the Palestinians if this should just happen to emerge as a result of negotiations among the countries in the area. This is a big 'if', since Israel is strong enough to block any outcome it dislikes. As of 1987, Canada's position was that it preferred an end to Israeli occupation of most of the West Bank and Gaza, to be replaced by a confederation of those regions with Jordan. Canada, furthermore, refuses to accept the Palestine Liberation Organization (PLO) as the sole legitimate spokesman for the Palestinians, even though public opinion polls show that 92.7 percent of the inhabitants of Gaza and the West Bank regard the PLO as their representative. Canada restricts contacts with the PLO to below the level of ambassador, a level lower than that maintained by most other Western Powers and the Vatican. Canada does accept that the Palestine Liberation Organization is a spokesman for the Palestinians. Canada's votes on Middle East issues in the United Nations usually follow the patterns set by Australia, Norway and New Zealand and rarely line up with those of Israel and the U.S. The U.S. and Israel standardly vote together and are almost invariably isolated on Middle East resolutions. Canada's votes, however, rarely support the world consensus on these issues and, like other American friends and allies, leave the impression in Arab eyes that we are camp followers of the Americans and Israelis.

Our policy, Ottawa claims, is one of balance, but most of our diplomats who have held responsibility for Middle East policy concur that the government of Canada has in fact been tilted towards Israel. This may cause surprise, since the Palestinians are the victims in this prolonged tragedy, and the Arabs have by far the most to offer Canada as trading partners. In 1948, the larger part of the Palestinians were driven out of their homes. Today, 3.45 million Palestinians have been scattered to many countries; 800,000 live as second-class citizens within Israel, most of them 15 years old and younger. Another 1.4 million are on the West Bank and in the Gaza Strip, under military rule that has now gone on for over twenty years.

Canadians have become increasingly supportive of human rights as an objective of their foreign policy. Our leaders, for example, boldly assert the rights of the black majority in South Africa, and the rights of Jews to emigrate from the Soviet Union. By comparison, they are decidedly restrained in their support of Palestinian rights. Why?

Most Canadians came to agree that the Jews, having suffered one of the worst crimes in all history at the hands of the Nazis persecution in several other European countries, and discrimination even in Canada, were entitled to an independent state of their own. The idea that it should be in the biblical homeland of the Jews appealed to many Canadians, most notably Pearson, who had been influenced by the Bible to believe that the Jews belonged in the "Holy Land" of Palestine. Little thought was given to the Palestinians, the people whose ancestors had been occupying the area for over thirteen hundred years. In the inevitable series of wars, and many lesser acts of violence, Canadian sympathy has generally been with the Israelis who appeared to be a tiny, "western" nation in grave danger of extinction at the hands of the hostile and much more numerous Arabs. That perception is changing. Israel has not only survived but expanded; its twenty year occupation of Gaza and the West Bank is rejected by the entire international community, including the United States. So too are its annexation of East Jerusalem and of the Golan Heights and its continued occupation of its "security zone" in South Lebanon. Israel's 1982 invasion of Lebanon evoked vigorous protest from such traditional friends as Canada.

Understanding of the Palestinian position has grown but is clouded by the impression, long fostered by the U.S.-Zionist propaganda disseminated by the media, that the PLO is little more than a terrorist gang dedicated to destroying Israel. The PLO has certainly employed guerilla warfare and terror tactics, and still does against targets inside Israel. Fringe elements within the PLO occasionally strike elsewhere. But the informed public knows that Jewish terrorism played an essential part in the displacement of Palestinians to make way for the influx of over a million refugees and immigrants. Former leaders of Jewish terrorist organizations are still prominent in Israeli public life. They include two recent prime ministers, Menachem Begin and Yitzhak Shamir, and Arik Sharon, the minister who directed the bloody invasion of Lebanon. Moreover, the Israeli bombing of refugee camps and villages, allegedly in retaliation, inflicts far greater suffering, with less discrimination, than the Palestinian attacks against Israeli civilian targets. Whatever one's sympathies, it is difficult to dispute the contention that the Middle East will remain a potential flash point for major war until the Palestinians receive partial justice in the form which makes their right to self-determination a reality on the West Bank and Gaza. There is no question of forcing Israel back from its pre-1967 borders to the area the 1947 UN Partition Plan allotted to the Jewish state. It will have to be given persuasive security guarantees by both the Palestinians and the world community.

A force of sanity is the growing awareness that the Palestinians, both within Israel and in the Occupied Territories, have a high birth rate which will bring their number close to that of the Israelis by the turn of the century. Ultimately Israel will have to relinquish control of the West Bank and Gaza, or grant Palestinians living there citizenship, thus destroying the Jewish-dominated character of the state, or impose a permanent system resembling South Africa's Apartheid. None of these prospects pleases the majority of Israelis at this point, but it remains difficult to muster the political will in Israel to negotiate seriously, still less to vacate the Occupied Territories.

The Palestinians are trapped in a catch 22 situation. If they adjust to Israeli rule, and concentrate on economic improvement, the world concludes that they are content with their lot and can be forgotten. If they employ violence, they will continue to be labelled "terrorists," needing to be kept under strict control.

The Palestinians have not always been assisted by their Arab brethren. Indeed they have at times been forcibly expelled from each of the neighbouring countries. Nevertheless, the knowledge that the Palestinian Arabs have either been driven from their ancestral home, or brought under alien rule, is deeply disturbing to all Arabs. The issue breeds hatred, not only against Israel, but also against the United States for defending Israel with its Security Council veto, and for supplying it with billions of dollars worth of the most sophisticated weapons. Sympathy for the Palestinians has become the touchstone of friendship with Arabs everywhere.

Canada sells no weapons to either party, votes more often than the U.S. to censure Israel, and speaks with a softer voice. One encounters in the Arab world less bitterness towards Canada than disappointment. However, when the Hon. Joe Clark, then Prime Minister, sought to move Canada's embassy in Israel from Tel Aviv to Jerusalem, this appeared to sanction Israel's conquest of the Holy Land. Anger throughout the Arab community was instantaneous, and effective; Clark backed off.

Most often Arabs attribute Canada's diplomatic tilt towards Israel to American pressure. We would be more sympathetic to them, they assume, if "Big Brother" would let us. This assumption hurts our image, even if it is largely false. Significant pressures on Ottawa accounting for the pro-Israel bias are domestic. They include the sympathies of many Canadians who view the Israelis as being Western, "like us," the active presence of a well-organized Israel lobby, and the absence of any comparable pro-Palestinian lobby.

Why should Canadians be concerned about this faraway quarrel between Israel and the Arabs? Trade diversification -- away from our dependence on the U.S. market -- is one reason for concern, especially as the Arabs are more interested in our products than are the Europeans or Japanese, and most of them have the means to pay. Another is tradition. Palestine is not only the place of origin of an active minority of our Arab-Canadian population, but the cradle of three world religions, including the one subscribed to by most Canadians. A more recent tradition derives from the outstanding Canadian contribution to the birth of Israel and the UN peace-keeping force necessary to deal with the turbulent consequences of that birth.

The greatest reason for concern lies in the potential of the Israeli-Palestine strife to spark a major war, perhaps one that would bring the two Cold War blocs into direct conflict. Israel itself is now a nuclear power. This fact puts pressure on those countries which are Israel's potential targets to develop and deploy credible deterrents, either in the form of their own nuclear weapons or in the form of chemical weapons of mass destruction.

What can Canada do about this danger? It can continue to provide troops for peace-keeping, and diplomatic effort to make it more effective. It can also continue to shift its voting in the United Nations so that it is in line with the world consensus. It can recognize the right of the Palestinians to self-determination, and the right of the PLO to speak for the Palestinians. Such steps would improve Canada's relations with the Arab world, and its image almost everywhere. But our influence would remain modest unless we join with other Commonwealth and European countries in efforts to persuade Israel and the U.S. to adopt different policies.

Canadians in the early years did not hesitate to make strong representations for peace through our close diplomatic channel to Washington, sometimes with success. We continue to do so on such issues as Central America, South Africa and arms control. The Middle East, by contrast, is almost never on the agenda when Canadian and American leaders meet. Our diplomats keep informed, but do not try seriously to influence American policy. Why not? Largely because the agenda of Canada-U.S. relations overflow with bilateral issues, such as trade and acid rain. Our diplomats are reluctant to risk irritating the Americans on matters, however critical, when there is no strong public or lobby pressure for action. Canada will not resume its modest but useful role in the troubled politics of the Middle East until Ottawa is made aware that a large number of voters are impatient with Canada's current passivity.

THE UNITED STATES, ISRAEL AND THE PALESTINIANS

Fouad Moughrabi

A kind of mystification or deliberate blindness has come to characterize analyses of United States policy toward Israel, the Palestinians, and the Arab World in general. In other areas of conflict such as Central America, the U.S. is seen as supporting horribly repressive regimes against the will of people searching for dignity and independence. In Southern Africa, again the United States has, by its actions, supported the apartheid system against the majority of African natives. In the Middle East, however, United States support for Israel has, until recently, been seen in a somewhat different light. Israel has successfully presented itself as a democracy fighting against attempts by the Arabs to destroy it. Furthermore, the Israelis have convinced a number of people that they are the target of a campaign of genocide by the Arabs and that this campaign aims at destabilizing the entire Western World on behalf of the Soviet Union. Israel is perceived as a reliable and strategic ally whose interests often coincide with America's interests and who is willing at all times to come to America's aid in the region and indeed throughout the world.

By contrast the Arabs in general have been painted in the media and in the cultural apparatus in the most negative and often racist manner. Muslims and Arabs have been labeled 'terrorists' and 'anti-Americans'. All Palestinians have also been labeled as terrorists who wish to destroy the Jewish state. Even solidly pro-American governments like Saudi Arabia and Jordan have not escaped this negative labeling. The American Congress has on repeated occasions refused to sell weapons to these countries, allegedly because they might be used to threaten Israel's security. These pro-American governments have been forced to turn to England and even the Soviet Union to buy the weapons they need to defend themselves against a possible threat from Iran.

The cloak of mystification surrounding Israel has begun to unravel in the last decade. Increasingly Israel is perceived very much in the same way as South Africa. A democracy for its Jewish citizens, it treats its Arab citizens as an alien and threatening community. The legal, socio-economic and political system discriminates against the Arabs in favour of the Jews. In Israel, for instance, there is one scale of justice for Jews and one for Arabs. As far as the occupied territories are concerned, Israel has been engaged in a process of force and beatings that has turned these Palestinian areas into places of misery and daily oppression.

In its basic outline, U.S. policy toward the Middle East differs very little from its approach to the Third World in general. The presence of a strong pro-Israel lobby has served the U.S. well -- it can claim that it is neutral were it not for the pressure of the lobby, or it can claim that it is powerless precisely because of it.

What are the strategic anchors of U.S. policy toward the Third World and especially toward the Middle East? In the first place, United States policy aims at securing areas where American interests, both economic and political, are guaranteed. Local friendly regimes are bolstered by economic and military assistance, even if these regimes have a notoriously bad record on human rights toward their own peoples. Threats to these regimes, both domestic and foreign, are dealt with in an overt manner by exerting political and economic pressure, or by covert means such as arming counter-revolutionary groups like the Contras, or the Unita faction in Angola or the Afghan rebels. Ideally, the United States prefers not to get involved directly by sending troops and usually relies on local proxies. In the best of circumstances, the U.S. would rather heavily subsidize a country which can serve as a local gendarme in the region. In Central America, no countries are able or willing to serve such a role. In the Middle East and Africa, however, both Israel and South Africa can serve such a role efficiently and economically. Israel has been willing to go even further, namely to serve as a conduit for U.S. assistance to discredited or unpopular groups throughout the world. Israel's involvement in the Iran-Contra scandal, its involvement with South Africa, and with various Central American dictatorships is by now quite well known.

Another strategic U.S. objective is to try to minimize Soviet influence in various parts of the world, especially in areas where such influence is marginal or contested. U.S. ability to reverse socialist gains in Central Europe, Vietnam, or Cuba is greatly limited. In the Middle East, however, Soviet influence was tenuous and therefore more easily reversed. Fighting Soviet influence has frequently been used as a cover for fighting local actors who may be rebelling against unjust treatment and exploitation, and whose victory may endanger friendly regimes. Nationalist movements struggling for freedom and dignity have nearly always been viewed as mere tools of the Soviet Union.

A third strategic anchor of U.S. diplomacy has been a consistent attempt to exclude the Europeans from various areas that the U.S. considers its own sphere of influence. The Middle East is a good example. In the 1950's American diplomacy was critical of the colonial powers (the British and the French). Later, the United States consistently refused to permit the European countries to be involved in the process of peace-making. In an attempt to secure the region for its own purposes, the United States tried to ensure its control of the flow of oil, its access to recycled petrodollars, its ability to sell its products in the region, and its control of the arms market. Other countries such as Japan and Canada have been similarly excluded from the process of peace-making, basically in an effort to diminish the possibility of increasing their trade and economic ties with the region.

Israel: A Strategic Ally or a Liability?

The prevailing sentiment within the American government, regardless of which party is in power, is that Israel is a reliable and strategic ally of the United States. Billions of dollars in economic and military assistance have gone to secure Israel's absolute dominance over its Arab neighbours. U.S. aid to Israel (currently running at $1.2 billion in economic aid and $1.8 billion in military assistance annually) constitutes nearly 11 per cent of Israel's gross national product and averages to approximately $600 per Israeli man, woman and child. This level of aid enables Israel to cover nearly one third of its defense budget. Israel is guaranteed nearly 100 million dollars in increases every year for the next fifteen years. No conditions are attached to this aid. In fact, the pressures resulting from the Gramm-Rudman Act to cut budgets has resulted in decreases in aid to most countries, except Israel. Furthermore, U.S. economic aid to Israel is not linked to any specific projects, a condition placed on every other recipient of U.S. foreign aid. In 1981, Congress converted all past economic aid to Israel to outright grants and forgiven loans; in 1985, military aid was likewise converted.

Until 1986, Israel used U.S. aid to subsidize the illegal settlements in the occupied West Bank and Gaza Strip. In 1986, however, the Agency for International Development pressured Israel to place U.S. funds in a separate account for better tracking purposes. Israel evaded the restriction on using aid to build settlements by using this money to free up other accounts, which then were used to establish settlements.

In spite of strong protectionist sentiments in Congress, Israel is permitted free access to U.S. markets. The Israeli defense industry has almost unlimited access to U.S. military technology. The Pentagon has recently approved a ten-year agreement granting Israel the same access to Pentagon contracts as America's NATO allies. In addition, Israel is permitted to further its own defense build-up by using U.S. aid money. Finally, the Pentagon has recently agreed to permit Israel to participate in SDI research to the tune of $1.2 billion for the design and manufacture of the Hetz, an antimissile missile.

A few Americans in public, and possibly more in private, doubt the wisdom of such unlimited largess, and the attempt to elevate U.S.-Israeli relations to such unprecedented levels. George Ball, who served as Under Secretary of State during the Kennedy and Johnson Administrations, argues that Israel lacks the key attributes of an ally of the United States. Ball says that the interests and the objectives of the two countries are far from congruent, that as a military ally Israel would offer America far greater disadvantages than benefits, and that Israel habitually fails to concert its policies with the U.S. or even consult before taking action. This special relationship will endanger American interests in the Arab World and may even put Israel at greater risk in the future.

U.S. foreign aid, which is Israel's lifeline, is decided by a Congress that is often willing to oblige. The pro-Israel lobby actively informs, rewards friends and punishes enemies. The level of political action committee (PAC) money given on behalf of pro-Israel groups exceeds the total amount contributed by the other most powerful lobbies in the U.S., such as the National Rifle Association and the American Medical Association. Pro-Israel PACs have donated at least $10.6 million in the last six years to favoured congressional candidates. This includes $2,088,133 as of June 30, 1988, in the current election cycle, $4.3 million in the 1986 election cycle, and at least $4.25 million in 1984. Congressmen who serve on the more important committees, such as the Armed Services and the Appropriations Committees of both houses, often get the lion's share of pro-Israel PAC contributions, regardless of whether they are Democrats or Republicans. Congressmen or senators who have less than a 100 percent record of voting on issues of importance to the lobby are sometimes targeted for defeat. Former Senator Charles Percy of Illinois, and congressmen Findley and McLoskey, were defeated mainly by contributions to their challengers from pro-Israel PACs.

The pro-Israel lobby has strength precisely because its objectives for Israel are defined in a manner to suit various important American constituencies. The principal group that benefits from close U.S.-Israel ties is, of course, the military-industrial complex. Aid to Israel has become closely intertwined with the defense budget. Furthermore, a rather hawkish position on East-West issues and on questions of arms control and detente is seen as potentially of benefit to Israel. Since there is such a ready consensus in favour of Israel in the U.S. Congress, it becomes easier to argue for constant increases in Defense Department allocations.

The United States and the Palestinians

Ever since the passage of U.N. Resolution 181 of 1947, that was designed to partition Palestine, and especially after the creation of the state of Israel in May 1948, the United States has limited itself to expressions of humanitarian interest in the fate of the Palestinian refugees. American diplomacy has supported Israel and Jordan, whose policies were designed from the very beginning to prevent at all cost the achievement of Palestinian statehood in the remaining part of Palestine. In this sense, American government hostility to Palestinian nationalism is not new. Nor is it any different from its hostility to other forms of nationalism in the Third World. Palestinian nationalism is perceived as hostile to the United States and a tool of Soviet aggression in the region.

By the late 1970's, an international consensus began to emerge as to the appropriate framework and modality of resolving what became known as the Palestinian-Israeli conflict. This consensus includes the following: a two state solution predicated on the principle of partition of the land between Jews and Arabs, mutual recognition of each other's right to self-determination, the recognition that the PLO speaks on behalf of the Palestinian people and should be represented in peace negotiations, and the convening of an international conference that would guarantee such a settlement.

Gradually, it appears that the American public has come to reflect this growing international consensus. Public opinion surveys over the last decade show that Americans are in favour of an independent state for the Palestinians by a two to one majority. Moreover, they support the participation of the PLO in peace talks, and the convening of an international peace conference. As a result of the Palestinian uprising, or **Intifada,** an even more significant shift in American public opinion has occurred. Not only does the public express criticism of Israel's harsh treatment of the Palestinians, but a significant portion of opinion leaders now endorse more supportive positions of the Palestinians.

U.S. government policy, however, has shifted hardly at all. It appears to be entrenched in the language of the post-1967 period, insisting that the Palestinians must recognize U.N. Resolutions 242 and 338 without any conditions, before they can be permitted to engage in peace talks. These resolutions fail to recognize the right of the Palestinian people to self-determination and call instead for a settlement of the conflict within the framework of negotiations between Israel and the neighbouring Arab states, especially Jordan. In the Camp David framework, the United States suggested autonomy for the Palestinians in association with Jordan. Autonomy means control over municipal affairs but not control over one's right to statehood. In 1982, President Reagan reiterated the Camp David formula and ruled out even more strongly the idea of a Palestinian state in the West Bank and Gaza. More recently, Secretary of State George Schultz reaffirmed this policy during his shuttle diplomacy in the region at the height of the Palestinian Uprising in March 1988.

In an attempt to respond to American and Israeli demands, the PLO has clarified its position even further, during the year of the Uprising. This process began with a statement by Bassam Abu Sharif, one of Arafat's key aides, which suggested a referendum in the Occupied Territories to determine, once and for all, whether the PLO had a mandate to negotiate on behalf of the Palestinians as their legitimate representative, urged direct talks between those representatives and Israel, re-iterated the PLO's acceptance of Security Council Resolutions 242 and 338 in the context of other relevant U.N. resolutions recognizing the national rights of the Palestinians, and accepted international guarantees for the security of all states in the region, including Palestine and Israel. On November 15, 1988, the Palestine National Council (PNC) declared an independent State of Palestine, basing its legitimacy under international law on the 1947 United Nations Resolution 181, partitioning Palestine into a Jewish and an Arab Palestinian state. The PNC thereby accepted the partition of Palestine and a two-state solution for the Israeli-Palestinian conflict. In its accompanying Political Statement, the PNC accepted the concept of an international peace conference based on 242 and 338 and the safeguarding of the legitimate national rights of the Palestinian people. On December 14, following his address to the U.N. General Assembly meeting held in Geneva, because the U.S. had denied him a visa to address the Assembly in New York, Chairman Arafat accepted the right of all parties concerned in the Middle East conflict to exist in peace and security, including the State of Palestine, Israel and other neighbours, according to Resolutions 242 and 338, and re-iterated the PNC's renunciation of all forms of terrorism, including individual, group and state terrorism. Within hours, the U.S., saying that Arafat has met their conditions for direct talks with the PLO, announced that it would begin a "substantive dialogue" with the PLO in Tunis for the first time. On December 15, however, the U.S. and Israel remained the only two countries voting against the General Assembly's resolution calling for an international peace conference on the

Middle East, supported for the first time by all of Western Europe. Only Canada and Costa Rica abstained. The U.S. continued to reject an independent Palestinian state and re-affirmed its strategic and "moral" commitment to Israel. Change may be in the air, but it will be slow in coming. Meanwhile the Palestinian Uprising in the West Bank and Gaza is still going strong. It is met with further escalations of repression by Israel. The death toll exceeds four hundred and the list of injured is now over forty-five thousand. Scores have been deported from their homes and thousands are held in administrative detention. Collective punishment, including the dynamiting of houses, is practised on a regular basis.

The United States has criticized Israel mildly on several occasions for the harshness of its handling of Palestinian unrest. No effective sanctions have been used to pressure Israel to alter its iron fist policy. Instead of reducing the amount of foreign aid given to Israel or linking the level of aid with Israel's behaviour, the United States has, in fact, increased economic and military aid to Israel.

The prospects for a significant change in U.S. policy toward the Palestinians do not appear promising. Eventually, however, the U.S. government will have to recognize the rights of the Palestinians to self-determination before any solution can be envisaged. At the moment there is no great incentive for the U.S. government to change its policy. The time may come when the cost to Israel and to the United States of maintaining the status quo will increase. At that point substantive changes will have to occur.

LOOKING TO THE UNITED NATIONS FOR SOLUTIONS

James A. Graff

How can the 40 year-old Palestinian-Israeli war be ended justly and humanely? Since 1983, there has been a growing consensus favouring a United Nations-sponsored international peace conference on the Middle East. By 1985, only Canada, Israel and the U.S. opposed such a conference, but Canada switched its official position in 1986, leaving only Israel and the U.S. opposed. Since then, the U.S. has given grudging support to the idea of a UN sponsored conference, and Israel's Foreign Minister and leader of her Labour Party, Shimon Peres, openly supported the idea by April, 1987. The Revolt of the Youth which started December 9, 1987 in Gaza gave new force to calls for such a conference, although Israeli Prime Minister Yitzhak Shamir has steadfastly opposed it and insisted that Israel will not surrender an inch of conquered territory. Nevertheless, many remain hopeful, since the only sensible and humane solution to the violence would have to be a negotiated, peaceful settlement accommodating both Palestinian aspirations and the security needs of Israel and her Arab neighbours.

There are major obstacles in the way of getting Israel to the negotiating table. Israeli majority public opinion supports Shamir's refusal to surrender an inch of occupied territory. The U.S. may give Peres verbal support but it is not prepared to drag Israel to the peace table. No one else, including Hussein, can accept the borders Shamir wants. Finally, there were three separate versions of a UN-sponsored international peace conference, each with its own guiding principles and format which jointly determine the outcome of each proposed conference. There could be no agreement on a conference because there was no agreement about an acceptable outcome. Until mid-1988, the only conference the U.S. would support is one which would guarantee the outcome it and Peres, for different reasons, could accept. That outcome is the "Jordanian Option", according to which Jordan would divide the West Bank and the Gaza Strip with Israel. It is an outcome which almost 93 percent of the Palestinians there firmly oppose, as does the PLO, which enjoys the support of slightly more than 93 percent of the Palestinians whose future is at stake. The Intifada unambiguously dramatized Palestinian opposition to "the Jordanian option". As a consequence, on July 31, 1988, King Hussein renounced Jordanian sovereignty over the West Bank. The "Jordanian option" now appears to be dead. The accommodation of Palestinian aspirations and of their right to political and social institutions of their own choosing on the West Bank and in Gaza are clearly embodied in the outcomes determined by the principles and format of the conferences called for by the UN General Assembly and the West Europeans.

For Peres and the U.S., no such outcome is acceptable. Rather they insist upon Security Council Resolutions 242 and 338 as the major guiding principles for their conference. Those resolutions refer to the Palestinians as refugees and therefore not as a people with a right to self-determination. The main resolution, 242 (November 22, 1967), "emphasizes" the principle of the inadmissibility of the acquisition of territory by force, calls for the "withdrawal of Israeli armed forces from territories occupied in the recent war," and "emphasizes" the need for secure and recognized borders for the then existing states in the region. Some interpret the resolution to require Israel's withdrawal from some, but not all of the territory it captured. Security Council Resolution 338 (October 22, 1973) calls for a cease-fire in the October War, urging all the parties to the conflict to implement 242. The implications of these resolutions are clearly that the negotiating parties are Israel, Egypt, Syria and Jordan. The PLO, which did not become a major player until after the 1967 war, would be effectively excluded from negotiations and there would be no acknowledgement of any right to self-determination for the Palestinian people. Whatever their fate, it would be sealed by agreements primarily between Jordan and Israel. The conference would provide a framework for direct state-to-state talks. The U.S., the Soviet Union and other Permanent Members of the Security Council would play largely ceremonial roles, opening the negotiations and sanctioning their outcomes. Israel would be recognized by the Arab states.

The conference the UN General Assembly envisions would establish an independent Palestinian entity on the West Bank and in Gaza. It would be established on principles Israel and the U.S. at present reject. In 1983, the General Assembly voted overwhelmingly for an international peace conference on the Middle East to which the Permanent Members of the Security Council, including the U.S. and the U.S.S.R., the Palestine Liberation Organization and the contending states would be invited to participate on an equal footing and with equal status. The vote was 123 in favour, 17 abstaining and 4 opposed. Australia, Canada, Israel and the U.S. cast the four negative votes. The NATO countries, New Zealand and a scattering of U.S. client states abstained. The resolution (38/58C) calls upon the Secretary General to convene an international peace conference which would proceed in conformity with a number of guidelines, including the right of the Palestinian people to self-determination and to return, the status of the Palestine Liberation Organization as the legitimate representative of the Palestinian people, withdrawal of Israel from territories occupied since 1967, acceptance of the principle of the inadmissibility of the acquisition of territory by force, and the invalidity under international law of Israel's annexation of East Jerusalem. It envisions a conference to which the permanent members of the Security Council, especially the U.S. and the U.S.S.R., would play active roles in negotiations aimed at a comprehensive regional settlement.

The outcome of this conference clearly would be an independent Palestinian state on the West Bank and in Gaza, an Israel confined mainly to its pre-1967 Green Line borders, superpower security guarantees and some arrangement for a general military step-down adequate to eliminate any serious risk of "pre-emptive" or other wars. What is aimed at is a really durable peace which would accommodate both the aspirations of the Palestinians for control over their own destiny and Israel's security needs within the context of military de-escalation. De-escalation would require agreements among the Great Powers over the supply of arms and material for the local manufacture of weapons. It would probably require cajoling or brow-beating the relevant states, including Israel, into accepting those arrangements which would undermine the power and status of their respective military elites and the commercial or industrial elites tied to them. It also calls for negotiations over the status of East Jerusalem which Israel has proclaimed "eternally" its own.

On February 23, 1987 the twelve Members of the European Economic Community issued a declaration stating that they favour an international conference under United Nations auspices "with the participation of the parties concerned and of any party able to make a direct and positive contribution to the restoration and maintenance of peace [in the Middle East] and to the region's economic and social development. The Twelve believe this conference should provide a suitable framework for the necessary negotiations between the parties directly concerned." The principles on which the conference should be based, are contained, the Declaration says, in the Venice Declaration of June 13, 1980. That Declaration lists two principles: "the right to existence and to security of all the states in the region, including Israel, and justice for all the peoples, which implies recognition of the legitimate rights of the Palestinian people." It goes on to state that: "A just solution must finally be found for the Palestinian problem, which is not simply one of refugees. The Palestinian people, which is conscious of existing as such, must be placed in a position, by an appropriate process defined

105

within the framework of the comprehensive peace settlement, to exercise fully its right to self-determination." It expressly states that the "Palestine Liberation Organization will have to be associated with the negotiations." It affirms the position that the settlements and modifications of population and of property in the occupied Arab territories are illegal under international law.

In March, the Nordic countries declared themselves in favour of a conference based on Security Council Resolutions 242 and 338, and on the right of the Palestinians to self-determination. The EEC/Nordic conferences, while not as fully accommodating Palestinian rights, would result in the emergence of some independent Palestinian political entity in most of the Occupied Territories.

From the point of view of acceptable outcomes, all but the U.S. and Israel could accept either the conference called for by 38/58C or the conference the EEC/Nordic countries have in mind. The crucial issues are 1) Palestinian self-determination, 2) the form of PLO representation and participation in negotiations, and 3) the roles, especially of the U.S. and the Soviet Union, in the negotiating process. The governments of the U.S. and Israel are the stumbling blocks to a genuine peace, because, for different reasons, neither would now accept any kind of really independent Palestinian entity in the Occupied Territories, and neither wants to see a genuinely demilitarized Israel. As it has been since 1967 and before, momentum towards peace is at an impasse, mainly because of what is going on in Israel and in Washington.

The Roots of the Impasse

An increasingly polarized Israeli society is divided into three ideological camps, each with its own image of what Israel is to be:

1)   Israel would be a Jewish-dominated, more or less openly Apartheid state whose borders include at least the presently occupied territories. In one form or another, this option enjoys the support of over 60 percent of Israel's Jewish electorate, roughly 18 percent of whom want to continue the status quo, 19 percent want outright annexation without expulsions, and 20.4 percent want to annex the territories and expel their Palestinian inhabitants. The expulsionist version of this vision is openly espoused by Rabbi Kahane, who has said that he would allow those Palestinians to stay who are prepared to serve as 'slaves' to the Jews; more "moderate" versions are espoused by Shamir, and Generals Sharon and Eitan.

2) Israel would be a state with separate and unequal development for Jewish and Arab sectors, ensuring Jewish domination and a Jewish majority fully enjoying democratic freedoms which would continue to be extended formally, but not effectively, to the Arab sector. This is basically the moderate and conservative Labour position represented by Peres. Support for this position, which is coupled with the "Jordanian Option" for the Occupied Territories, has ranged as high as 37 percent and appears to have fallen to about 31 percent within the Jewish electorate.

3) Israel would be a fully democratic state, promoting equal development of its Jewish and Arab sectors, co-incident with integrating the Arab sector fully into Israel's political and economic institutions. Israel's borders would reflect some minor adjustments of the 1967 Green Line and Israel would scale-down its military establishment in a process leading to full integration as one state among others in the Middle East. This is the vision of Israel as basically the state of its citizens and not the state of the Jewish nation whose in-gathering requires Lebensraum. It is the vision represented by former General Matti Peled and the Progressive List for Peace, by left-Labour, most of Mapam and a scattering of others on the Left. It has never enjoyed more than 9 percent support within the Jewish electorate.

Supporters of the "centre" position have cause for growing concern that they may be marginalized by electoral victories by the basically anti-democratic, expansionist majority. Some in the Centre are beginning to have serious concerns that they, like a handful of Jews promoting the third image, may suffer prosecution and persecution. That explains Peres' efforts to get some settlement, but it also explains his rejection of an independent Palestinian entity. Such an entity is overwhelming rejected by the Jewish electorate. It would be an ideological "dagger pointed at the heart of (his) Israel."

For its part, present U.S. strategy appears to require an Israel threatened by and threatening its neighbours. Such an Israel sustains the type of insecurity and instability which permits the U.S. to win and hold the "friendship" of powerful Arab military elites in poor and rich countries alike. In the poor countries, a combination of military sales and aid ensure dependence for security and for the regime's survival against its domestic revolution. The nature and scope of economic aid which is not aimed at significant economic development, coupled with the burdens of maintaining large military establishments, also help to sustain economic dependence on the U.S. This strategy requires external threats where there are no serious domestic threats, and is advanced where there are. It is a strategy which favours military and commercial elites in the Arab countries and Israel's military-industrial elites. A similar strategy where economic aid is replaced by sales of U.S. technology and expertise, applies to the relatively few oil-rich Arab states. Economic dependence is bolstered by sales of technology and services, and by encouraging enormous capital investments in the U.S. Those investments tie their owners closer to the U.S. economy and therefore to U.S. interests. Israel's dependence is underscored by the fact that its economy would collapse without the yearly U.S. subsidies, now reaching the equivalent of $1400 U.S. for every man, woman and child there. Unlike dependent Arab states, however, Israel has a powerful lobby in the U.S. which it can rely on to insulate it from American pressures when Israeli and American interests or objectives conflict.

The U.S. government's strategy of control is aimed at securing well-known American economic and strategic objectives in the region: access to oil, to Arab markets, and containing Soviet influence. It is also aimed at containing Western European influence and subordinating European policies there to perceived American interests.

Peace in the Middle East requires a major re-thinking in Washington and in Israel of the character of those respective states, the one as World and the other as Regional superpower. It requires a re-evaluation of the modalities by which influence can be exercised and sustained without domination and dependence. It would require each, no doubt, to settle for less economically and politically, than it presently enjoys.

A Note on Canada

Canada deserves at least a footnote in this discussion, partly because that is precisely where our Government has placed us. Only in early June, 1987 did Joe Clark align Canada with the call for an international peace conference under United Nations auspices, stating that Canada "strongly supports" the efforts of Hussein and those of other Middle East leaders (i.e., Peres, Mubarak and King Hassan) to convene such a conference. His language was vague enough to permit Canada to support the EEC's versions of the conference and its outcome, or to support the Peres-U.S. line. Since then, Prime Minister Mulroney at the September Francophone Summit in Quebec City refused to join the consensus recognizing the right of the Palestinians to self-determination. This meant that only Canada, Israel, South Africa and the U.S. refuse to recognize that right. It also meant that Canada was isolated from the rest of the Commonwealth and Western Europe on the issue. Canada seems to have lined up with the Peres-Washington version of a peace conference and with the "Jordanian Option." In January 1988, during the Palestinian uprising, Jordan declared that it was not interested in a conference that would exclude the PLO or fail to accept the right of the Palestinians to self-determination. Egypt followed with a similar public stand. By the end of April, 1988, the U.S. had mounted a series of high-profile efforts supporting the Peres/Washington version of the UN-sponsored conference. Prominent Palestinians, however, continued to insist on PLO representation and on their right to self-determination, while Prime Minister Shamir adamantly rejected any UN-sponsored peace conference. Canada's position was thrown into confusion by King Hussein's renunciation of sovereignty over the West Bank. On December 15, 1988, only Canada and Costa Rica abstained on the General Assembly's call for an international peace conference on the Middle East. The U.S. and Israel alone voted against the call, but every other country of the world supported it. Canada remained not-so-splendidly isolated, not quite with the U.S. and Israel, but also, not with what had become a nearly unanimous world consensus.

Options

The Israelis, who have the guns and troops in the West Bank and Gaza, and enjoy American diplomatic and financial support, have a limited number of options:
1) They can annex the West Bank and Gaza. If they do, they will be confronted with a Palestinian majority soon after the year 2,000. This would threaten exclusive Jewish control of the Israeli state and economy unless they impose a kind of Apartheid system. They could expel masses of Palestinians (a programme favoured now by 20.4 percent of Jewish Israelis). Finally, they could extend democratic rights to Palestinians, but that would effectively create a bi-national state and de-Zionize Israel, an outcome still ideologically unpalatable to all but 10 percent of Jewish Israelis. The Palestinians under occupation oppose all three options. If one gives weight to their rights, none of these options is morally acceptable.
2) They can withdraw from part of almost all of the West Bank and Gaza. This would require a negotiated settlement. Peres' preferred option is to negotiate with Jordan to have it take over control of

about 60 percent of the West Bank, while Israel controls the rest in a patchwork quilt of settlements. Presumably, Gaza would fall under a similar arrangement. But the Palestinians oppose rule by Jordan and again, if one gives weight to their rights, this solution would be morally unacceptable. It would also be inherently unstable.

3) Finally, they could negotiate with genuine representatives of the Palestinians and work out a settlement the Palestinians and the Israelis could live with. This seems the only morally acceptable option, but it remains the one which, to date, the overwhelming majority of Jewish Israelis oppose. There are, however, an increasing number of prominent Israelis, including some of the right wing, who have come to accept this option.

Peace is not likely to break out soon.

ISLAM: FAITH AND PRACTICE

Mahmoud Ayoub

Rise of Islam and Its Early History

Islam is the third monotheistic religion to emerge in the Near East, after Judaism and Christianity. There were in northern Arabia, the birthplace of Islam, sizeable Jewish and Christian communities which had influenced the moral and religious ideas of Arab society. Perhaps pagan Arabs before Islam had learned from their Christian and Jewish neighbours about the one and supreme creator God whom Arabic-speaking Jews and Christians called by His Arabic name: Allah, meaning, "the God". Although pre-Islamic Arabs recognized Allah as the supreme God, they still worshipped many idols.

In 570 or 571 A.D., in the city of Mecca in northern Arabia, the Prophet of Islam, Muhammad son of Abdallah, was born. He grew up an orphan, and was cared for first by his grandfather, and when he died, by his uncle. Muhammad was of the tribe of Quraysh, which enjoyed considerable power and prestige among the neighbouring Arab tribes.

Although Arabia, by and large, was a nomadic, pastoral society organized on tribal lines, Mecca was an important centre of trade and commerce. Sitting astride the caravan routes over which the spices of southern Arabia and other products travelled northwards to Syria and beyond, and eastward to Mesopotamia and Persia, it had grown in wealth and power. Its influence was enhanced by the fact that it was the home of the ancient shrine of the Kaabah, which at that time housed idolatrous images and attracted large crowds to its annual pilgrimage. The religion of Islam, therefore, was not the product of a purely nomadic, desert environment, as some people have thought. Rather it was born in an important urban centre.

At the age of forty, around 612 A.D., Muhammad was, according to Islamic tradition, called by God to be a prophet to his people, and to humankind. Thus he began to preach faith in God, and to call people to worship God alone instead of idols. He also preached kindness, especially to one's close relatives, to the poor, the orphan and the wayfarer. This universal message of "submission (islam) to God" and kindness to others is contained in the Qur'an, the Scripture of Islam.

In Mecca, Muhammad and his few poor followers were at first rejected and persecuted by the men of the Quraysh. Still, they patiently went on preaching the new faith and worshipping God together. In 622 A.D., the Prophet and some of his fellow Muslims left Mecca and migrated to Medina, where they established the first Islamic state. After ten years of hard struggle and negotiation, the Prophet and his fellow immigrants entered Mecca, and all its inhabitants accepted Islam. The Prophet Muhammad died two years after Mecca accepted Islam, and ten years after the migration (hijrah) to Medina, 10 A.H./632 A.D.

Following the death of the Prophet, Islam spread rapidly into Asia, Africa and Europe. The Muslims were ruled by a caliph, or successor, to the Prophet. The enlarged Islamic state thus included many people of high civilizations and major religious traditions. It was also neighbour to Byzantium from which Muslim scholars acquired a deep knowledge of ancient Greek philosophy and science. In Baghdad, the capital of the Muslim state and great centre of learning, one of the caliphs, al-Ma'mun, built in the ninth century the first great university of the Middle East, which he called "The House of Wisdom". There, Muslim, Jewish and Christian scholars studied, translated and commented on the works of ancient Greek philosophers, physicians, mathematicians and scientists. These scholars also wrote their own books on these and other important subjects.

The Muslims ruled southern Spain and Sicily for centuries. Muslim philosophy, medicine, music, and the sciences were transmitted to the West from the universities of Baghdad and Cairo, and those of Cordova and Seville and other cities of southern Spain. This creative interaction between the Christian and Islamic civilizations was one of the primary causes of their greatness. Islam took from the West philosophy and science, and in turn deeply influenced the European Renaissance and the rise of the scientific and industrial age.

Faith and Practice

The word islam, as already observed, means submission or faith-commitment to the will of God. A follower of Islam is called a Muslim. The principles of Islamic faith are contained in the Qur'an, the Islamic scripture, which Muslims believe was revealed to the Prophet Muhammad over a period of some twenty years.

The fundamentals of Islam are: faith in the One God, in His Books (principally the Torah, the Gospel and the Qur'an), in His messengers (foremost among whom are Abraham, Moses, Jesus, and Muhammad), in His angels, and in the Day of Judgment. Islam rests on what is known as "The Five Pillars of Islam". These are the affirmation or testimony (shahadah), "There is no god but God"; the five daily prayers; the fast of the month of Ramadan; the obligatory aims or welfare tax (zakat); and, at least once in a person's life-time, the pilgrimage (hajj) to Mecca.

The social, moral and religious life of the Muslim community is regulated by the Shari^{C}ah, or Islamic sacred law. The sources of Islamic law are: the Qur'an, the life-example (Sunnah) of the Prophet, analogical and rational deduction (ijtihad) of the jurists, and finally the general consensus (ijma^C) of the community. The Shari^{C}ah is the framework within which marriage and divorce, buying and selling, and legal and criminal judgments are executed.

Islam is a comprehensive way of life, meant not only for the individual alone, but for society at large. The Qur'an, for this reason, stipulates harsh punishments for public crimes such as stealing, adultery and murder. Its primary aim is to reform human society and preserve public order and social integrity. Thus it often enjoins repentance and pardon instead of such punishments.

Women in pre-Islamic Arabia had no individual rights. In fact, in cases where a family had too many girls, female infants were sometimes buried alive. Islam strictly prohibited this practice and gave the woman the right to inherit and own property, and dispose of it as she wishes. It also gave her the right to choose her marriage partner.

There are now nearly a billion Muslims in the world, many thousands of whom live in Canada. As Muslims accept the Prophets of Judaism and Christianity, and because they share with these two communities faith in the One God, Muslims, Jews, and Christians in Canada can and should live as good neighbours and cooperate in the service of God and society. Jews, Christians and Muslims have generally lived as good neighbours in the past, being all "the children of Abraham"; there is no doubt that in a multi-cultural and multi-religious society like Canada, they can recreate that earlier period of cultural creativity and good neighbourliness.

CHRISTIANS IN THE ARAB WORLD

Habib Salloum

A good number of people in the West would be astonished to know that there are some 11,500,000 Christians residing in the Arab countries. Yet, the ancestors of these followers of Christ have lived in that part of the world since the first days of Christianity. The direct descendants of the original adherents to the Cross, they are virtually unknown to their co-religionists in the Western World.

Even though Muslims have been portrayed as fanatics who offered the conquered people Islam or the sword, these ancient Christians have lived among them in relative peace. Many times down through history friction arose when some Christians were manipulated by foreign powers. This happened most flagrantly during the Crusades, and in the 19th and 20th centuries when the European powers used the native Christians as pawns to pave the way for their control of the Middle Eastern lands, thus helping to foster Muslim intolerance.

Under Islamic law, Christians were termed <u>ahl al-kitab</u> (people of the Book who possessed a validly revealed religion). As such, even though they did not have true equality, they lived in the Muslim state as a protected minority, provided they paid the <u>jizya</u> (protection tax) in lieu of military service.

This degree of tolerance was much better than that accorded the Jews in Christian Europe and often much better than that accorded the Muslims under Christian rulers. A good example of this was manifested in the <u>reconquista</u> of Spain when the Muslims were forcibly converted to Christianity, executed or expelled from the country. There is no better testimony to Muslim tolerance than the host of Christian sects which today are to be found in every corner of the Middle Eastern Arab lands. A short look at these venerable churches will give one an idea of how Christianity has thrived and is still flourishing in its land of origin.

<u>Greek Orthodox</u>

The Greek Orthodox Church is the original Church of the Holy Land. It was founded by Saint Paul, preaching among the Greek-speaking townspeople in the Middle East. About 40 A.D., Antioch (in northern Syria) became the headquarters of the newly established

114

religion, and Greek the language of the Church. However, in the last few centuries, Arabic has gradually replaced Greek.

In its early history the Church established four Patriarchates: Antioch, Jerusalem, Alexandria and Constantinople -- all of which still exist. In the ensuing centuries other national units of this Church were formed in Greece, Russia and a number of Balkan countries. In our times, as Antioch is no longer a city of importance, the Patriarch of Antioch, who controls the 600,000 followers of the Church in Syria and Lebanon, resides in Damascus.

In the Fertile Crescent, a good number of the Christians still belong to this Church, the bulk of them in Syria where about 10 percent of the population is Christian. The majority are proud of their Arab heritage and consider themselves part of the Arab nation. Many prominent Arabs in Syria, Jordan, Lebanon and the Palestine area belong to this first church in Christianity.

The Coptic Church

The Copts of Egypt, who are Monophysites, are said to number about 8,500,000, and are the largest Christian sect in the Middle East. The name 'Copt' is derived from the Arabic pronunication of the Greek name for Egypt. Christianity became popular in Egypt during the first three centuries of our era and the Patriarch of Alexandria was one of the four great prelates of the Christian church. As an independent church with an important Abyssinian branch, it has stood the test of centuries.

During the past century, the Copts occupied a prominent place in commerce, education and the professional fields in Egypt, and under the British occupation of the country they were favoured by the occupying power. Due to the loss of this privileged position, coupled with a widespread sense of discrimination felt by the Christians of Egypt in recent times, a good number of them have immigrated to Canada and the United States.

The Syrian Orthodox or Jacobite Church

The Jacobite Monophysite Church was founded by Jacob Baradaeus during the 7th century in Antioch.

Unlike the Greek Orthodox Church which developed in the urban centres, the Jacobite Church had its roots in the countryside where the Syriac tongue was dominant. Hence, Syriac became the principal language of the Jacobite rituals. From the time of the Crusades until the

First World War, the Patriarchs of the Church made a monastery near Mardin in modern day Turkey their headquarters. When after the War most of the Christians were expelled from Turkey for co-operating with the Allies, the Patriarchate was moved to Homs, then to Damascus in Syria.

Today, the membership of the Church, which is about 130,000, is concentrated in the Jazirah region of Syria, northern Iraq and southeast Turkey. In addition, the Church controls the large community of Jacobites on the Malabar Coast of India.

The Nestorian Church

The Nestorians are the followers of Nestorius who was appointed Patriarch of Constantinople in 428 A.D. His teachings that there were two persons in Christ instead of the one person officially recognized, led to his being condemned and his followers thereafter created a separate church. Persecution pushed the Nestorians to the East and in the interior of Asia, where Islam held sway, the Church became popular and influential. It was favoured by the Muslim rulers and during the golden age of Islam it played a prominent role in the formation of Arab culture.

Now known as Assyrians, the followers of Nestorius, who currently number about 200,000, are to be found in northern Iraq and along the Khabbur River in Syria. They still use Aramaic, the language of Christ, for their rituals.

The National Armenian or Gregorian Church

The Armenian Gregorian Church was established about 300 A.D. It followed the Monophysite doctrine and when this was condemned by the Orthodox Church, it broke away and formed an independent national Church. Its centre, which was for centuries in modern day Turkey, led to a tragic history. After siding with Russia during the First World War, the Armenians were persecuted and expelled from their ancient homeland by the Turks. Those who survived made their way to Syria and Lebanon, aided by Arab bedouin tribes. Today, they form influential communities of some 200,000 in these two countries.

The Catholic Churches

After the Roman Catholic Church separated from the Greek Orthodox Church in 1045 A.D., it set out to win converts from the oriental churches. It has succeeded through the centuries in converting, in whole or part, many of the eastern sects. Most of the affiliated churches have been allowed to keep their own rituals and the right to use the vernacular languages, as well as allowing priests to marry.

The Maronite Church

The Maronite Church is perhaps the most important of these autonomous churches. Its name goes back to John Maro, its first Patriarch, who died in 707 A.D. Followers of this church came originally from northern Syria and settled in the impregnable fastness of the mountains in north Lebanon. They started out as Monothelites, who believed that Christ had two natures in one person, but only one will. When the Crusaders came, the Maronites supported them, and in 1182 A.D. they united with the Roman Catholic Church. However, they were allowed to keep their own rituals and the Syriac language.

Their Patriarch resides in Bkirki, Lebanon and is a member of the Catholic College of Cardinals. The membership of the Church is about 800,000, found mainly in Syria and Lebanon.

Other Catholic Churches of the East which are allowed to keep their own rituals are: the Greek Catholic or Melkite Church with 400,000 members; the Chaldean Catholic Church with 200,000 members; the Syrian Catholic Church with 80,000 members; the Coptic Catholic Church with 15,000 members; and the Armenian Catholic Church.

The Protestant Churches

There are now a considerable number of Protestant churches in the Middle East as a result of conversions by European and American missionaries. These are concentrated in Egypt, Syria, Lebanon and the Palestine area. Presbyterians, Anglicans, Methodists, Adventists and almost all other Protestant sects have members scattered throughout these countries.

Most of the congregations in all these churches are former members of the eastern sects. Few Muslims have been converted.

117

With the spread of education and the revival of the ancient churches, fewer are leaving to join the missionary churches.

Conclusion

Most of these Christian groups are represented in Jerusalem -- Christianity's most holy city and the third most holy city in Islam. These Christian sects together form a sizeable minority of the Palestinian people, at least 10-12 percent.

All the eastern churches have thousands of followers in almost every country of the Americas and, to some extent, in Australia. The emigrants in the majority of cases have not left their mother churches. Rather, they have greatly helped to revitalize the ancient churches of their fathers, especially with financial aid.

For most of the eastern churches, the future looks bright. A number of these, like the Greek Orthodox and Melkite Churches, have to a large extent supported Arab nationalism and, hence, their members are accepted by the Muslims as part of Middle Eastern society. On the other hand, those who still look to the West for inspiration and protection, like the Maronites and some of the Protestant Churches, are having a difficult time. Foreign intervention on their behalf, from the Crusaders to the modern Israelis, has always brought problems and, at times, ruin to their followers.

SOME KEY DOCUMENTS

THE BASEL PROGRAMME
August, 1897

The aim of Zionism is to create for the Jewish people a home in Palestine secured by public law.

In order to obtain this object the Congress adopts the following means:
1. The systematic promotion of the settlement of Palestine with Jewish agriculturalists, artisans and craftsmen.
2. The organization and federation of all Jewry by means of local and general institutions in conformity with the local laws.
3. The strengthening of Jewish sentiment and national consciousness.
4. Preparatory steps for the procuring of such government assents as are necessary for achieving the object of Zionism.

* * * * *

BALFOUR DECLARATION
November 2, 1917

Dear Lord Rothschild,

I have much pleasure in conveying to you, on behalf of His Majesty's Government the following declaration of sympathy with Jewish Zionist aspirations which has been submitted to, and approved by, the Cabinet.

"His Majesty's Government view with favour the establishment in Palestine of a national home for the Jewish people, and will use their best endeavours to facilitate the achievement of this object, it being clearly understood that nothing shall be done which may prejudice the civil and religious rights of existing non-Jewish communities in Palestine, or the rights and political status enjoyed by Jews in any other country."

I should be grateful if you would bring this declaration to the knowledge of the Zionist Federation.

Lord Arthur James Balfour

* * * * *

THE LAW OF RETURN

The "Law of Return" was passed unanimously by the Knesset on July 5, 1950 and written into the State Legislation.

The Law of Return states:

1. Every Jew has the right to immigrate to the country.
2. (a) Immigration shall be on the basis of immigration visas.
    (b) Immigrant visas shall be issued to any Jew expressing a desire to settle in Israel, except if the Minister of Immigration is satisfied that the applicant:
    (i) acts against the Jewish nation; or
    (ii) may threaten the public health or State security.
3. (a) A Jew who comes to Israel and after his arrival expresses a desire to settle there may, while in Israel, obtain an immigrant certificate.
    (b) The exceptions listed in Article 2 (b) shall apply also with respect to the issue of an immigrant certificate, but a person shall not be regarded as a threat to public health as a result of an illness that he contracts after his arrival in Israel.
4. Every Jew who migrated to the country before this law goes into effect, and every Jew who was born in the country either before or after the law is effective enjoys the same status as any person who migrated on the basis of this law.
5. The Minister of Immigration is delegated to enforce this law and he may enact regulations in connection with its implementation and for the issue of immigrant visas and immigrant certificates.

* * * * *

PALESTINIAN NATIONAL CHARTER
As revised by the 4th Palestine National Council Meeting, July 1968
(Extracts)

1. Palestine is the homeland of the Arab Palestinian people; it is an indivisible part of the Arab homeland, and the Palestinian people are an integral part of the Arab nation.
2. Palestine, with the boundaries it had during the British Mandate, is an indivisible territorial unit.
3. The Palestinian Arab people possess the legal right to their homeland and have the right to determine their destiny after

achieving the liberation of their country in accordance with their wishes and entirely of their own accord and will.

4. The Palestinian identity is a genuine, essential, and inherent characteristic; it is transmitted from parents to children. The Zionist occupation and the dispersal of the Palestinian Arab people, through the disasters which befell them, do not make them lose their Palestinian identity and their membership in the Palestinian community, nor do they negate them.

5. The Palestinians are those Arab nationals who, until 1947, normally resided in Palestine regardless of whether they were evicted from it or have stayed there. Anyone born, after the date, of a Palestinian father -- whether inside Palestine or outside it -- is also a Palestinian.

6. The Jews who had normally resided in Palestine until the beginning of the Zionist invasion will be considered Palestinians.

7. That there is a Palestinian community and that it has a material, spiritual, and historical connection with Palestine are indisputable facts. It is a national duty to bring up individual Palestinians in an Arab revolutionary manner. All means of information and education must be adopted in order to acquaint the Palestinian with his country in the most profound manner, both spiritual and material, that is possible. He must be prepared for the armed struggle and ready to sacrifice his wealth and his life in order to win back his homeland and bring about its liberation.

8. The phase in their history, through which the Palestinian people are now living, is that of national struggle for the liberation of Palestine. Thus the conflicts among the Palestinian national forces are secondary, and should be ended for the sake of the basic conflict that exists between the forces of Zionism and of imperialism on the one hand, and the Palestinian Arab people on the other. On this basis the Palestinian masses, regardless of whether they are residing in the national homeland or in diaspora, constitute -- both their organizations and the individuals -- one national front working for the retrieval of Palestine and its liberation through armed struggle.

9. Armed struggle is the only way to liberate Palestine. Thus it is the overall strategy, not merely a tactical phase. The Palestinian Arab people assert their absolute determination and firm resolution to continue their armed struggle and to work for an armed popular revolution for the liberation of their country and their return to it. They also assert their right to normal life in Palestine and to exercise their right to self-determination and sovereignty over it.

10. Commando action constitutes the nucleus of the Palestinian popular liberation war. This requires its escalation, comprehensiveness, and the mobilization of all the Palestinian popular and educational efforts and their organization and involvement in the armed Palestinian revolution. It also requires the achieving of unity for the national struggle among the different groupings of the Palestinian people, and between the Palestinian people and the Arab masses, so as to secure the continuation of the revolution, its escalation, and victory.

11. The Palestinians will have three mottoes: national unity, national mobilization, and liberation.

12. The Palestinian people believe in Arab unity. In order to contribute their share toward the attainment of that objective, however, they must, at the present stage of their struggle, safeguard their Palestinian identity and develop their consciousness of that identity, and oppose any plan that may dissolve or impair it.

13. Arab unity and the liberation of Palestine are two complementary objectives, the attainment of either of which facilitates the attainment of the other. Thus, Arab unity leads to the liberation of Palestine, the liberation of Palestine leads to Arab unity; and work towards the realization of one objective proceeds side by side with work toward the realization of the other.

14. The destiny of the Arab nation, and indeed Arab existence itself, depend upon the destiny of the Palestine cause. From this interdependence spring the Arab nation's pursuit of, and striving for, the liberation of Palestine. The people of Palestine play the role of the vanguard in the realization of this sacred national goal.

15. The liberation of Palestine, from an Arab viewpoint, is a national duty and it attempts to repel the Zionist and imperialist aggression against the Arab homeland, and aims at the elimination of Zionism in Palestine. Absolute responsibility for this falls upon the Arab nation -- peoples and governments -- with the Arab people of Palestine in the vanguard. Accordingly, the Arab nation must mobilize all its military, human, moral, and spiritual capabilities to participate actively with the Palestinian people in the liberation of Palestine. It must, particularly in the phase of the armed Palestinian revolution, offer and furnish the Palestinian people with all possible help, and material and human support, and make available to them the means and opportunities that will enable them to continue to carry out their leading role in the armed revolution, until they liberate their homeland.

16. The liberation of Palestine, from a spiritual point of view, will provide the Holy Land with an atmosphere of safety and tranquility, which in turn will safeguard the country's religious sanctuaries and guarantee freedom of worship and of visit to all, without discrimination of race, color, language, or religion. Accordingly, the people of Palestine look to all spiritual forces in the world for support.

17. The liberation of Palestine, from a human point of view, will restore to the Palestinian individual his dignity, pride and freedom. Accordingly the Palestinian Arab people look forward to the support of all those who believe in the dignity of man and his freedom in the world.

18. The liberation of Palestine, from an international point of view, is a defensive action necessitated by the demands of self-defense. Accordingly, the Palestinian people, desirous as they are of the friendship of all people, look to freedom-loving and peace-loving states for support in order to restore their legitimate rights in Palestine, to re-establish peace and security in the country, and to enable its people to exercise national sovereignty and freedom.

19. The partition of Palestine in 1947 and the establishment of the state of Israel are entirely illegal, regardless of the passage of time, because they were contrary to the will of the Palestinian people and to their natural right in their homeland, and inconsistent with the principles embodied in the Charter of the United Nations, particularly the right to self-determination.

20. The Balfour Declaration, the Mandate for Palestine, and everything that has been based upon them, are deemed null and void. Claims of historical or religious ties of Jews with Palestine are incompatible with the facts of history and the true conception of what constitutes statehood. Judaism, being a religion, is not an independent nationality. Nor do Jews constitute a single nation with an identity of its own; they are citizens of the states to which they belong.

21. The Arab Palestinian people, expressing themselves by the armed Palestinian revolution, reject all solutions which are substitutes for the total liberation of Palestine and reject all proposals aiming at the liquidation of the Palestinian problem, or its internationalization.

22. Zionism is a political movement organically associated with international imperialism and antagonistic to all action for liberation and to progressive movements in the world. It is racist and fanatic in its nature, aggressive, expansionist, and colonial in its aims, and fascist in its methods. Israel is the instrument of the Zionist

movement, and a geographical base for world imperialism placed strategically in the midst of the Arab homeland to combat the hopes of the Arab nation for liberation, unity, and progress. Israel is a constant source of threat via-à-vis peace in the Middle East and the whole world. Since the liberation of Palestine will destroy the Zionist and imperialist presence and will contribute to the establishment of peace in the Middle East, the Palestinian people look for the support of all the progressive and peaceful forces and urge them all, irrespective of their affiliations and beliefs, to offer the Palestinian people all aid and support in their just struggle for the liberation of their homeland.

23. The demands of security and peace, as well as the demands of right and justice, requires all states to consider Zionism an illegitimate movement, to outlaw its existence, and to ban its operations, in order that friendly relations among peoples may be preserved, and the loyalty of the citizens to their respective homelands safeguarded.

24. The Palestinian people believe in the principles of justice, freedom, sovereignty, self-determination, human dignity, and in the right of all peoples to exercise them.

25. For the realization of the goals of this Charter and its principles, the Palestine Liberation Organization will perform its role in the liberation of Palestine in accordance with the Constitution of this Organization.

26. The Palestine Liberation Organization, representative of the Palestinian revolutionary forces, is responsible for the Palestinian Arab people's movement in its struggle -- to retrieve its homeland, liberate and return to it and exercise the right to self-determination in it -- in all military, political, and financial fields and also for whatever may be required by the Palestine case on the inter-Arab and international levels.

27. The Palestine Liberation Organization shall cooperate with all Arab states, each according to its potentialities; and will adopt a neutral policy among them in the light of the requirements of the war of liberation; and on this basis it shall not interfere in the internal affairs of any Arab state.28.   The Palestinian Arab people assert the genuineness and independence of their national revolution and reject all forms of intervention, trusteeship, and subordination.

29. The Palestinian people possess the fundamental and genuine legal right to liberate and retrieve their homeland. The Palestinian people determine their attitude toward all states and forces on the basis of the stands they adopt vis-à-vis the Palestinian case and the extent of

the support they offer to the Palestinian revolution to fulfill the aims of the Palestinian people.

30. Fighters and carriers of arms in the war of liberation are the nucleus of the popular army which will be the protective force for the gains of the Palestinian Arab people.

31. The Organization shall have a flag, an oath of allegiance, and an anthem. All this shall be decided upon in accordance with a special regulation.

32. Regulations, which shall be known as the Constitution of the Palestine Liberation Organization, shall be annexed to this Charter. It shall lay down the manner in which the Organization, and its organs and institutions, shall be constituted; the respective competence of each; and the requirements of its obligations under the Charter.

33. This Charter shall not be amended save by [vote of] a majority of two-thirds of the total membership of the National Congress of the Palestine Liberation Organization [taken] at a special session convened for that purpose.

* * * * *

DECLARATION OF INDEPENDENCE
November 15, 1988
(Excerpts)

Palestine, the land of the three monotheistic faiths, is where the Palestinian Arab people was born, on which it grew, developed and excelled. The Palestinian people was never separated from or diminished in its integral bonds with Palestine. Thus the Palestinian Arab people ensured for itself an everlasting union between itself, its land and its history....

And it was the Palestinian people, already wounded in its body, that was submitted to yet another type of occupation over which floated the falsehood that "Palestine was a land without people". This notion was foisted upon some in the world, whereas in Article 22 of the Covenant of the League of Nations (1919) and in the Treaty of Lausanne (1923), the community of nations had recognized that all the Arab territories, including Palestine, of the former Ottoman Empire were to have been granted their freedom as provisionally independent nations.

Despite the historical injustice inflicted on the Palestinian Arab people resulting in their dispersion and depriving them of their right to self-determination, following upon U.N. General Assembly Resolution 181 (1947), which partitioned Palestine into two states -- one Arab, one Jewish -- yet it is this Resolution that still provides those conditions of international legitimacy that ensure the right of the Palestinian Arab people to sovereignty and national independence.

By stages, the occupation of Palestine and parts of other Arab territories by Israeli forces, the willed dispossession and expulsion from their ancestral homes of the majority of Palestine's civilian inhabitants was achieved by organized terrorism; those Palestinians who remained, as a vestige subjugated in its homeland, were persecuted and forced to endure the destruction of their national life.

Thus were principles of international legitimacy violated. Thus were the Charter of the United Nations and its Resolutions disfigured, for they had recognized the Palestinian Arab people's national rights, including the right of Return, the right of independence, the right to sovereignty over territory and homeland....

The massive national uprising, the Intifada, now intensifying in cumulative scope and power on occupied Palestinian territories, as well as the unflinching resistance of the refugee camps outside the homeland, have elevated consciousness of the Palestinian truth and right into still higher realms of comprehension and actuality. Now at last the curtain has been dropped around a whole epoch of prevarication and negation. The Intifada has set siege to the mind of official Israel, which has for too long relied exclusively upon myth and terror to deny Palestinian existence altogether. Because of the Intifada and its revolutionary irreversible impulse, the history of Palestine has therefore arrived at a decisive juncture.

Whereas the Palestinian people reaffirms most definitively its inalienable rights in the land of its patrimony:

Now by virtue of natural, historical and legal rights, and the exercise of these rights, and the sacrifices of successive generations who gave of themselves in defence of the freedom and independence of their homeland;

In pursuance of Resolutions adopted by Arab Summit Conferences and relying on the authority bestowed by international legitimacy as embodied in the Resolutions of the United Nations Organization since 1947;

and in exercise by the Palestinian Arab people of its rights to self-determination, political independence, and sovereignty over its territory;

126

The Palestine National Council, in the name of God, and in the name of the Palestinian Arab people, hereby proclaims the establishment of the State of Palestine on our Palestinian territory with its capital Jerusalem (Al-Quds Ash-Sharif).

The State of Palestine is the state of Palestinians wherever they may be. The state is for them to enjoy in it their collective national and cultural identity, theirs to pursue in it a complete equality of rights. In it will be safeguarded their political and religious convictions and their human dignity by means of a parliamentary democratic system of governance, itself based on freedom of expression and the freedom to form parties. The rights of minorities will duly be respected by the majority, as minorities must abide by decisions of the majority. Governance will be based on principles of social justice, equality and non-discrimination in public rights, on grounds of race, religion, colour or sex under the aegis of a constitution which ensures the rule of law and an independent judiciary. Thus shall these principles allow no departure from Palestine's age-old spiritual and civilizational heritage of tolerance and religious co-existence.

The State of Palestine is an Arab state, an integral and indivisible part of the Arab nation, at one with that nation in heritage and civilization, with it also in its aspiration for liberation, progress, democracy and unity. The State of Palestine affirms its obligation to abide by the Charter of the League of Arab States, whereby the cooperation between the Arab States shall be strengthened. It calls upon Arab compatriots to consolidate and enhance the emergence in reality of our State, to mobilize potential and resources, and to intensify efforts to end Israeli occupation.

The State of Palestine proclaims its commitment to the principles and purposes of the United Nations, and to the Universal Declaration of Human Rights. It proclaims its commitment as well to the principles and policies of the Non-Aligned Movement.

Announcing itself to be a peace-loving State adhering to the principles of peaceful co-existence, it will join with all states and peoples in order to assure a permanent peace based upon justice and the respect of rights so that humanity's potential for well-being may be assured, an earnest competition for excellence be maintained, and confidence in the future achieved for those who are just and for whom justice is the only recourse.

In the context of its struggle for peace in the Land of Love and Peace, the State of Palestine calls upon the United Nations to bear special responsibility for the Palestinian Arab people and its homeland. It calls upon all peace- and freedom-loving peoples and states to assist it in the attainment of its objectives, to provide it with security, to alleviate the tragedy of its people, and to help it terminate Israel's occupation of the Palestinian territories.

The State of Palestine herewith declares that it believes in the settlement of regional and international disputes by peaceful means, in accordance with the U.N. Charter and resolutions. Without prejudice to its natural right to defend its territorial integrity and independence, it therefore rejects the threat or use of force, violence and terrorism against its territorial integrity or political independence, as it also rejects their use against the territorial integrity of other states....

Therefore, we call upon our great people to rally to the banner of Palestine, to cherish and defend it, so that it may forever be the symbol of our freedom and dignity in that homeland, which is a homeland for the free, now and always.

* * * * *

POLITICAL STATEMENT OF THE PALESTINE
NATIONAL COUNCIL
November 15, 1988
(Excerpts)

Reinforcing the steadfastness of our people and our Intifada and responding to our people within the occupied homeland and outside it, and in fidelity to the memory of our martyrs and our wounded, the P.N.C. decides:

First: On the escalation and continuation of the Intifada;

A. To provide all means for intensifying the Intifada in every aspect and in every way;

B. To strengthen the support of popular institutions and organizations within the occupied Palestinian lands;

C. To reinforce and develop popular committees, organizations and union leaders to assure their effectiveness, including attack groups and the popular army;

D. To consolidate the national unity manifested by the Intifada;

E. To intensify efforts at the international level for the release of detainees, for the return of those expelled, and for an end to repression and organized terrorism against our children, women and men as well as against our institutions;

F. To call on the United Nations to place occupied Palestinian territory under international supervision to protect our masses and end the Israeli occupation;

G. To call on the Palestinian people outside the homeland to intensify and increase their support to needy families within the occupied territories;

H. To call on the Arab nations and its peoples, forces, institutions, and governments to increase their political, financial and media support for the Intifada;

I. To call on free men and women all over the world to stand beside our people and our revolution and to oppose the Israeli occupier, his repressive measures and his fascist militarily organized terrorism, which is carried out by forces of the occupation army and by armed, fanatical settlers, against our people, universities, schools, institutions, and our sacred places of worship, Christian as well as Moslem.

Second: In the political field,

Proceeding from all the above, the Palestine National Council -- on the basis of its responsibility toward our Palestinian people, its national rights, and its desire for peace on the basis of the Declaration of Independence issued on November 15, 1988, and responding to a humanitarian desire to try to reinforce international detente and nuclear disarmament and the settlement of regional disputes by peaceful means -- affirms the determination of the Palestine Liberation Organization to reach a comprehensive peaceful solution of the Arab-Israeli conflict and its essence, the Palestinian cause, within the framework of the United Nations charter, the principles and provisions of international legitimacy, the rules of international law, the resolutions of the United Nations (the latest being United Nations Security Council Resolutions 605, 607 and 608), and the resolutions of the Arab Summits in a manner that assures the right of the Palestinian Arab people to return, exercise self-determination, and establish its independent national state on its national territory, and create arrangements of security and peace for all the states of the region.

To implement this, the Palestine National Council affirms:

1. The necessity of holding an effective international conference concerning the Middle East issue and its essence, the Palestinian cause, under the auspices of the United Nations and with the participation of the permanent member states of the United Nations Security Council and all the parties to the struggle in the region,

including the Palestine Liberation Organization, the sole legitimate representative of the Palestine people, on an equal footing, and by considering that the international conference will be held on the basis of United Nations Security Council Resolutions 242 and 338 and the assurance of the legitimate national rights of the Palestinian people and, first and foremost, their right to self-determination in application of the principles and provisions of the United Nations charter concerning the right of peoples to self-determination and the inadmissibility of seizing the lands of others by force or military invasion, and in accordance with the resolutions of the United Nations regarding the Palestinian and Arab territories that it has been occupying since 1967, including Arab Jerusalem.

2. Israeli withdrawal from all the Palestinian and Arab territories that it has occupied since 1967, including Arab Jerusalem.
3. Annulment of all measures of annexation and attachment; and removal of the settlements that Israel has established in the Palestinian and Arab territories since the year 1967.
4. An effort to place the occupied Palestinian territories, including Arab Jerusalem, under the supervision of the United Nations for a limited period to protect our people and to create an atmosphere favorable to insuring the success of the proceedings of the International Conference; the attainment of a comprehensive peaceful solution, and the achievement of security and peace for all through mutual acceptance and satisfaction, and to enable the Palestinian state to exercise its effective authority over these territories.
5. Settlement of the issue of the Palestinian refugees in accordance with the resolutions of the United Nations regarding this matter.
6. The guarantee of the right to worship and the exercise of religious rites at the holy places in Palestine for the followers of all religions.
7. The Security Council will draw up and guarantee the arrangements for security and peace among all the affected states in the region, including the Palestinian state.

* * * * *

UNITED NATIONS RESOLUTIONS

<u>United Nations General Assembly Resolution 181 (II) Concerning the Future Government of Palestine, November 29, 1947</u>

The General Assembly ...

PART I
FUTURE CONSTITUTION AND GOVERNMENT OF PALESTINE

A. TERMINATION OF MANDATE, PARTITION AND INDEPENDENCE

1. The Mandate of Palestine shall terminate as soon as possible but in any case not later than 1 August, 1948,
2. The armed forces of the mandatory Power shall be progressively withdrawn from Palestine, the withdrawal to be completed as soon as possible but in any case not later than 1 August, 1948. ... the mandatory Power shall use its best endeavours to ensure that an area situated in the territory of the Jewish State, including a seaport and hinterland adequate to provide facilities for a substantial immigration, shall be evacuated at the earliest possible date, and in any event, not later than 21 February, 1948.
3. Independent Arab and Jewish States and the Special International Regime for the City of Jerusalem, set forth in Part III of this plan, shall come into existence in Palestine two months after the evacuation of the armed forces of the mandatory Power has been completed, but in any case, not later than 1 October 1948. The boundaries of the Arab State, the Jewish State and the City of Jerusalem shall be described in Parts II and III below.

B. STEPS PREPARATORY TO INDEPENDENCE (summarized)

1. A Commission shall be set up consisting of one representative of each of five Member States. The members represented on the Commission shall be elected by the General Assembly ....
2. The administration of Palestine shall, as the mandatory Power withdraws its armed forces, be progressively turned over to the Commission; which shall act in conformity with the recommendations of the General Assembly, under the guidance of the Security Council.
3. On its arrival in Palestine the Commission shall proceed to carry out measures for the establishment of the frontiers of the Arab and Jewish States and the City of Jerusalem in accordance with the general lines of the recommendations of the General Assembly on the partition of Palestine ....

4.   The Commission, after consultation with the democratic parties and other public organizations of the Arab and Jewish States, shall select and establish in each State as rapidly as possible, a Provisional Council of Government. The activities of both the Arab and Jewish Provisional Councils of Government shall be carried out under the general direction of the Commission.

 If by 1 April 1948 a Provisional Council of Government cannot be selected by either of the States, or, if selected, cannot carry out its functions, the Commission shall communicate that fact to the Security Council for such action with respect to that State as the Security Council may deem proper ....

5.   Subject to the provisions of these recommendations, during the transitional period the Provisional Councils of Government, acting under the Commission, shall have the full authority in the areas under their control, including authority over matters of immigration and land regulation.

[The Commission was to have progressively passed over its powers to the Provisional Councils of Government of the two States. In fact, the Commission never had any authority.]

7.   The Commission shall instruct the Provisional Councils of Government of both the Arab and Jewish States, after their formation, to proceed to the establishment of administrative organs of government, central and local.

8.   The Provisional Council of Government of each State shall, within the shortest time possible, recruit an armed militia for the residents of that State, sufficient in number to maintain internal order and to prevent frontier clashes.

 This armed militia in each State shall, for operational purposes, be under the command of Jewish or Arab officers resident in that State, but general political and military control, including the choice of the militias' high command, shall be exercised by the Commission.

9.   The Provisional Council of Government of each State shall, not later than two months after the withdrawal of the armed forces of the mandatory Power, hold elections to the Constituent Assembly which shall be conducted on democratic lines.

 ... Qualified voters for each state for this election shall be persons over 18 years of age who are: a) Palestinian citizens residing in that State and b) Arabs and Jews residing in the State, although not Palestinian citizens, who, before voting, have signed a notice of intention to become citizens of such a State.

Arabs and Jews residing in the City of Jerusalem who have signed a notice of intention to become citizens, the Arabs of the Arab State and the Jews of the Jewish State, shall be entitled to vote in the Arab and Jewish States respectively.

Women may vote and be elected to the Constituent Assemblies.

During the transitional period no Jew shall be permitted to establish residence in the area of the proposed Arab State, and no Arab shall be permitted to establish residence in the area of the proposed Jewish State, except by special leave of the Commission.

10. [Calls for the drafting of a democratic constitution with a representative legislature for each of the two States, and the establishment of a provisional government.

The constitution shall provide for:]

    b) Settling all international disputes in which the State may be involved by peaceful means in such a manner that international peace and security, and justice, are not endangered;

    c) Accepting the obligation of the State to refrain in its international relations from the threat or use of force against the territorial integrity or political independence of any state, or in any other manner inconsistent with the purposes of the United Nations;

    d) Guaranteeing to all persons equal and non-discriminatory rights in civil, political, economic and religious matters and the enjoyment of human rights and fundamental freedoms, including freedom of religion, language, speech and publication, education, assembly and association;

    e) Preserving freedom of transit and visit for all residents and citizens of the other State in Palestine and the City of Jerusalem, subject to considerations of national security provided that each State shall control residence within its borders.

11. The Commission shall appoint an economic commission of three members to make whatever arrangements are possible for economic co-operation, with a view to establishing, as soon as practicable, the Economic Union and the Joint Economic Board as provided in section D below.

C.   DECLARATION

A declaration shall be made to the United Nations by the provisional government of each proposed State before independence. It shall contain inter alia the following clauses:

GENERAL PROVISION

The stipulations contained in the declaration are recognized as fundamental laws of the State and no law, regulation or official action shall conflict or interfere with these stipulations, nor shall any law, regulation or official action prevail over them.

CHAPTER I

Holy Places, religious buildings and sites

1. Existing rights in respect of Holy Places and religious buildings or sites shall not be denied or impaired.
2. In so far as Holy Places are concerned, the liberty of access, visit and transit shall be guaranteed, in conformity with existing rights, to all residents and citizens of the other State and of the City of Jerusalem, as well as to aliens without distinction as to nationality, subject to requirements of national security, public order and decorum ....
3. Holy Places and religious buildings or sites shall be preserved. No act shall be permitted which may in any way impair their sacred character.

CHAPTER II

Religious and minority rights

1. Freedom of conscience and the free exercise of all forms of worship, subject only to the maintenance of public order and morals, shall be ensured to all.
2. No discrimination of any kind shall be made between the inhabitants on the grounds of race, religion, language or sex.
3. All persons within the jurisdiction of the State shall be entitled to equal protection of the laws.
4. The family law and personal status of the various minorities and their religious interests, including endowments, shall be respected.
6. The State shall ensure adequate primary and secondary education for the Arab and Jewish minority, respectively, in its own language and its cultural traditions.

The right of each community to maintain its own schools for the education of its own members in its own language, while conforming to such educational requirements of a general nature as the State may impose, shall not be denied or impaired. Foreign educational establishments shall continue their activity on the basis of their existing rights.

7. No restriction shall be imposed on the free use by any citizen of the State of any language in private intercourse, in commerce, in religion, in the Press or in publications of any kind, or at public meetings. [A footnote stipulates that: "In the Jewish State, adequate facilities shall be given to Arabic-speaking citizens for the use of their language, either orally or in writing, in the legislature, before the Courts and in the administration."]

8. No expropriation of land owned by an Arab in the Jewish State (by a Jew in the Arab State) shall be allowed except for public purposes: In all cases of expropriation, full compensation as fixed by the Supreme Court shall be paid previous to dispossession.

CHAPTER III

Citizenship, International Conventions and financial obligations

1. Citizenship.
    Palestinian citizens residing in Palestine outside the City of Jerusalem, as well as Arabs and Jews who, not holding Palestinian citizenship, reside in Palestine outside the City of Jerusalem shall, upon the recognition of independence, become citizens of the State in which they are resident and enjoy full civil and political rights ....

PART II
BOUNDARIES
(the boundaries are shown in the Partition Plan Map)

PART III
CITY OF JERUSALEM
(boundaries were extended to include Bethlehem)

PART IV
(Deals with the rights of foreign nationals prior to partition and their rights after partition)

* * * * *

General Assembly Resolution 194 (III) Concerning the Progress Report of the United Nations Mediator, December 11, 1948

(Established a Conciliation Commission consisting of three member states of the UN, to assume the functions of the assassinated UN Mediator on Palestine, Count Folk Bernadotte. The Commission consisted of France, Turkey and the U.S. The resolution declared that there should be free access to the Holy Places, including Nazareth, that the City of Jerusalem should be placed under UN authority, and required that refugees be allowed to return and that compensation be given to those who chose not to return to the Jewish controlled areas.)

The General Assembly,

11. Resolves that the refugees wishing to return to their homes and live at peace with their neighbours should be permitted to do so at the earliest practicable date, and that compensation should be paid for the property which, under principles of international law or in equity, should be made good by the governments or authorities responsible;

    Instructs the Conciliation Commission to facilitate the repatriation, resettlement and economic and social rehabilitation of the refugees and the payment of compensation, and to maintain close relations with the Director of the United Nations Relief for Palestine Refugees and, through him, with the appropriate organs and agencies of the United Nations;

* * * * *

General Assembly Resolution 273 (III) Admitting Israel to Membership in the United Nations, May 11, 1949

... Recalling its resolutions of 29 November 1947 [see Partition Resolution, 181 above] and 11 December 1948 [see Resolution 194 above], and taking note of the declarations and explanations made by the representative of the Government of Israel before the ad hoc Political Committee in respect of the implementation of the said resolutions,

The General Assembly,

Acting in discharge of its functions under Article 4 of the Charter and Rule 125 of its Rules of Procedure

1. Decides that Israel is a peace-loving state which accepts the obligations contained in the Charter and is able and willing to carry out those obligations;
2. Decides to admit Israel to membership in the United Nations.

* * * * *

SECURITY COUNCIL RESOLUTIONS

S.C. 242 (November 22, 1967)

Expressing its continuing concern with the grave situation in the Middle East,

Emphasizing the inadmissibility of the acquisition of territory by war and the need to work for a just and lasting peace in which every state in the area can live in security,

Emphasizing further that all member states in their acceptance of the Charter of the United Nations have undertaken a commitment to act in accordance with Article 2 of the Charter,

1. Affirms that the fulfillment of Charter Principles requires the establishment of a just and lasting peace in the Middle East which should include the application of both the following principles:
    I. Withdrawal of Israeli armed forces from territories occupied in the recent conflict;
    II. Termination of all claims or states of belligerency and respect for and acknowledgement of sovereignty, territorial integrity and political independence of every state in the area and their right to live in peace within secure and recognized boundaries free from threats or acts of force;
2. Affirms further the necessity
    a) For guaranteeing freedom of navigation through international waterways in the area;
    b) For achieving a just settlement of the refugee problem;
    c) For guaranteeing the territorial inviolability and political independence of every state in the area, through measures including the establishment of demilitarized zones;
3. Requests the Secretary General to designate a special representative to proceed to the Middle East to establish and maintain contacts with the states concerned in order to promote agreement and assist efforts to achieve a peaceful and accepted settlement in accordance with the provisions and principles in this resolution;

4. Requests the Secretary General to report to the Security Council on the progress of the efforts of the special representative as soon as possible.

* * * * *

S.C. 338 (October 22, 1973)

The Security Council
1. Calls upon all parties to the present fighting to cease all firing and terminate all military activity immediately, no later than 12 hours after the moment of the adoption of this decision, in the positions they now occupy;
2. Calls upon the parties concerned to start immediately after the cease-fire the implementation of Security Council Resolution 242 (1967) in all its parts;
3. Decides that immediately and concurrently with the cease-fire, negotiations start between the parties concerned under appropriate auspices aimed at establishing a just and durable peace in the Middle East.

* * * * *

Summary of General Assembly Resolution 38/58C, 13 December 1983

The General Assembly: Recalling 36/120C, calling for an International Peace Conference under UN auspices, and 37, reiterating the UN's responsibility to strive for a lasting peace in the Middle East through a just solution of the problem of Palestine,
2. endorses the Geneva Declaration on Palestine of 7 September, 1983,
3. welcomes and endorses the call for an International Peace Conference on the Middle East in conformity with the following guidelines:
    a) The attainment by the Palestinian people of its legitimate inalienable rights, including the right to return, the right to self-determination, and the right to establish its own independent state in Palestine;
    b) The right of the Palestine Liberation Organization, the representative of the Palestinian people, to participate on an

equal footing with other parties in all efforts, deliberations and conferences on the Middle East;

c) The need to put an end to Israel's occupation of the Arab territories in accordance with the principle of inadmissibility of the acquisition of territory by force, and, consequently, the need to secure Israeli withdrawal from the territories occupied since 1967, including Jerusalem;

d) The need to oppose Israeli policies and practices in the Occupied Territories which contravene international law or UN resolutions;

e) The need to reaffirm as null and void all Israeli legislation purporting to alter the status or character of Jerusalem or of property therein;

f) The right of all States in the region to existence within secure and internationally recognized boundaries, with justice and security for all the people, the sine qua non of which is the recognition and attainment of the legitimate, inalienable rights of the Palestinian people as stated in paragraph (a) above;

4. Invites all parties to the Arab-Israeli conflict, including the Palestine Liberation Organization, as well as the United States of America, the Union of Soviet Socialist Republics, and other concerned States, to participate in the International Peace on the Middle East on an equal footing and with equal rights;

5. Request the Secretary General, in consultation with the Security Council, urgently to undertake preparations for the Conference;

6. Invites the Security Council to facilitate arrangements for the Conference;

7. Also requests the Secretary General to report on his efforts no later than March 15, 1984; and

8. Decides to consider the Secretary General's report on the Conference at the 39th General Assembly Session.

IVTH GENEVA CONVENTION
August 12, 1949

EXTRACTS OF AND COMMENTS ON ARTICLES RELATING TO ISRAELI PRACTICES IN THE OCCUPIED TERRITORIES

James A. Graff

Israel, Canada and many other countries have signed this Convention. Canada and almost every other country of the world hold that it applies to Israel's occupation of the West Bank, the Gaza Strip, East Jerusalem and the Golan Heights. Israel does not do so, and consequently does not recognize as violations most of the practices listed below. Israel does claim to uphold relevant sections of the Convention, supplemented by British Emergency Regulations, and by its interpretations of existing Turkish or Jordanian law. The Convention requires an occupying power to respect existing law within the territories it occupies so long as that law is not inhumane.

In the articles, the term "protected person" refers to anyone who finds him/herself "in the hands" of a foreign country which has seized the territory they inhabit by force of arms (Article 4). Thus every inhabitant of a conquered territory or country is a "protected person."

Article 27:

> "Protected persons are entitled, in all circumstances, to respect for their persons, their honour, their family rights, their religious convictions and practices, and their manners and customs. They shall at all times be humanely treated, and shall be protected especially against all acts of violence or threat thereof and against insults and public curiosity."

There have been attacks on persons and their property by extremist right wing Jewish "settlers" which have gone largely unpunished and uninvestigated. Palestinian youths suspected of throwing stones, participating in protest demonstrations, or other "security offenses" are frequently beaten, subjected to insults or humiliations by Israeli soldiers. Both the apparent official "blind eye" and leniency towards Jewish "settler" violence and the aforementioned practices of Israeli troops, prison authorities and border police, when documented, are cited as examples of violations of Article 27.

Article 31:

> "No physical or moral coercion shall be exercised against protected persons, in particular to obtain information from them or from their parties."

During the interrogations of "security suspects", Israeli authorities often use beatings, sometimes torture, and various harsh methods to extract "confessions" or accusations against other Palestinians. Such practices clearly violate Article 31.

Article 33:

> "No protected person may be punished for an offense he or she has not personally committed. Collective penalties and likewise all measures of intimidation or of terrorism are prohibited.
> "Pillage is prohibited.
> "Reprisals against protected persons and their property are prohibited."

Israeli authorities have demolished homes or sealed the family homes of security suspects as a form of "collective punishment." They have used curfews to confine the Palestinian residents of towns, villages and refugee camps to their homes for days as a means of punishing a community for demonstrations or stone-throwing by some of their members. They have also closed schools and universities for extended periods of time in retaliation for protests, stone-throwing or other security offenses by students. These practices violate Article 33.

Article 42:

> "The internment or placing in assigned residence of protected persons may be ordered only if the security of the Detaining Power makes it absolutely necessary."

Although some detentions certainly conform to the requirements of this Article, it would be fair to say that most do not. Many detentions are for short periods of time, without trial. Students are sometimes arrested without charge to keep them from writing crucial entrance or final examinations. Since 1967, over a quarter of a million Palestinians, mainly males between the ages of 15 and 25, have been detained. Many of these detentions have involved beatings, insults and humiliations. Round-ups of youths following an incident are commonplace.

Article 47:

> "Protected persons who are in occupied territory shall not be deprived, in any case or in any manner whatsoever, of the benefits of the present Convention by any change introduced, as the result of the occupation of a territory, into the institutions or government of the said territory, or by any agreement concluded between the authorities of the occupied territory and the Occupying Power, nor by any annexation by the latter of the whole or part of the occupied territory."

Israel's annexations of East Jerusalem and of the Golan Heights, and its expropriation of over 50 percent of the land of the West Bank and 30 percent of the land of the Gaza Strip violate this Article.

Article 49 (1):

> "Individual or mass forcible transfers, as well as deportations of protected persons from occupied territory to the territory of the Occupying Power or to that of any other country, occupied or not, are prohibited regardless of their motive."

Israel's practice of expelling Palestinians from the Occupied Territories to foreign countries violates this Article.

Article 49 (6):

> "The Occupying Power shall not deport or transfer parts of its own civilian population into the territory it occupies."

Israel's settlement of nearly 70,000 Jewish Israelis in the West Bank, and 2,000 in Gaza in "Jewish only" colonies violate this Article.

So too does the much larger settlement of Jewish Israelis in East Jerusalem.

Article 53:

> "Any destruction by the Occupying Power of real or personal property belonging individually or collectively to private persons or to the State, or to other public authorities, or to social or co-operative organizations, is prohibited, except where such destruction is rendered absolutely necessary by <u>military operations</u>."

The practice of demolishing homes as punishment or to make way for Jewish Israeli colonies in the Occupied Territories are among the practices violating this Article.

BIBLIOGRAPHY

A. Basic Texts

American Friends Service Committee. A Compassionate Peace: a
Future for the Middle East. New York: Hill & Wang, 1982.
242 p. $5.95 pap.
Pursues the quest for reconciliation and a turn from
violence; examines the various ongoing struggles from
Lebanon and Palestine to Iran and Afghanistan, Great Power
involvement, the politics of oil, arms sales, etc.; aims at a
descriptive and unbiased account and reasonable solutions.

Chomsky, Noam. The Fateful Triangle: the United States, Israel
and the Palestinians. Boston: South End press, 1983.
481 p. $10.00 pap.
An examination of U.S. policies and its special
relationship with Israel, including its diplomatic support, its
massive economic aid, including the financing of Israeli
settlements in the Occupied Territories, the supply of arms,
etc.; probes into several Arab-Israeli wars and the prospect of
a final Armageddon in the area; incisive and convincing.

Chomsky, Noam. Pirates and Emperors. Montreal; New York:
Black Rose Books, 1987. 174p. pap.
An altogether different perspective on the international
terror network, especially as this pertains to the Middle East.
A distinction is made between "retail terror" which is
perpetrated by small groups (pirates) and "wholesale terror"
which is perpetrated by nations (emperors) like the U.S. and
Israel. Through an analysis of specific events such as the
U.S. bombing of Libya and the Israeli invasion of Lebanon,
the author shows how the 'emperors' have, through a
manipulation of the media and the language of terror,
succeeded in covering up their terrorist acts while concurrently
attributing all terrorism to the 'retail terrorist'.

144

Epp, Frank and John Goddard. The Palestinians: Portrait of a People in Conflict. Toronto: McClelland and Stewart, 1976. 204 p. $10.00.
  Gives an intimate picture of the Palestinians in their homes in Israel, the Occupied Territories and the refugee camps; based on recorded interviews on successive visits; good photography, charts and maps; "a valuable document of great immediacy and impact."

Flappan, Simha. The Birth of Israel: Myths and Reality. New York: Pantheon Books, 1987. 277 p. $27.75.
  A courageous book utilizing Israeli and Arab sources, comparing both with the historical record, by someone within the Zionist experience who became national secretary of the Mapam Party and head of its Arab Affairs Department; a radical revision of the mythology upon which the State of Israel is founded; indispensable to an understanding of the conflict and the road to an eventual peace.

Hirst, David. The Gun and the Olive Branch: the Roots of Violence in the Middle East. London: Faber and Faber, 1977; Futura Publications repr., 1983. 367 p. £2.50.
  Begins with the "seeds of conflict" prior to the British Mandate, traces the subsequent growth of violence by both sides and records in some detail the events of the five Arab-Israeli Wars down to the findings of the Kahan Commission of Inquiry into the Sabra and Shatila massacres in Lebanon; factual, thorough, aimed at redressing the "overwhelming Zionist sympathies" of American literature on the Palestinian-Zionist struggle.

Jiryis, Sabri. The Arabs in Israel, trans. by Inea Bushnaq; forword by N. Chomsky. New York/London: Monthly Review Press, 1976; first published in Hebrew, 1966. 314 p. $12.50 pap.
  A carefully documented study of the second-class status of the Arab minority in Israel in their subjugation to military rule for 18 years; details the confiscation of their land, the Kfar Kassim massacre of 1956, and the political, social and economic disabilities under which they live.

145

Khalidi, Walid, ed. <u>From Haven to Conquest</u>. Beirut: Institute for Palestine Studies, 1971.

 An anthology which deals with the Zionist claims to land ownership and immigration to Palestine, focusing on Biblical Palestine up to 1948. Brings together Arabic, Hebrew, French, German and other sources not usually accessible to the English-speaking reader.

Ingram, Doreen. <u>Palestine Papers 1917-1922: Seeds of Conflict</u>. London: John Murray, 1972. 198 p.

 Based on revealing British documents from Lord Balfour's Declaration of 1917 to Churchill's first White Paper of 1922, and of Chaim Weizmann and Prince Faisal; invaluable for an understanding of how decisions were made and policy formulated in this crucial period.

Langer, Felicia. <u>With my own Eyes: Israel and the Occupied Territories, 1967-1973</u>. London: Ithaca press, 1975. 166 p. £3.80, £2.50 pap.

 The story by an Israeli lawyer of how she sought to defend the human and civil rights of the Palestinians; deals with the confiscation of property, deportations, the blowing up of homes, the torture of prisoners; an eye opener.

Said, Edward W. <u>The Question of Palestine</u>. New York: Vintage Press, 1979/London: Routledge & Kegan Paul, 1980. 265 p. £7.50 pap.

 A distinguished scholar and member of the Palestinian National Council portrays the living experiences of a dispossessed people, relentlessly pursued, subject to derogation and the denial of their peoplehood; illuminates the Palestinian reality, the development of Palestinian self-consciousness, and what Camp David has meant to them.

Said, E.W., I. Abu-Lughod, J.L. Abu-Lughud, M. Hallaj and E. Zureik. <u>A Profile of the Palestinian People</u>. Prepared for and published by the Palestine Human Rights Campaign, 1983. 29 p.

 A concise and comprehensive summary of the history and political development of the Palestinian people, their institutions and their organizations; an excellent introduction for an understanding of the Palestinian predicament.

Shehadeh, Raja. Occupier's Law: Israel and the West Bank. Prepared for Law in the Service of Man, the West Bank affiliate of the International Commission of Jurists. Washington, D.C.: Institute for Palestine Studies, 1985. 212 p. pap.

Documents the various legal methods used by the Israeli occupiers to take over land on the West Bank at the expense of the human and civil rights of the Palestinians, resulting in "creeping annexation"; shows how the Palestinians are at the mercy of the judicial system, the military government and the Israeli settlers.

B. For Further Reading and Reference

Abu Lughod, Ibrahim, ed. Palestinian Rights: Affirmation and Denial. Wilmette, Ill.: Medina Press, 1982. 225 p. $7.95 pap.

Composed of papers given at four seminars organized by the UN Committee on the Exercise of the Inalienable Rights of the Palestinian People, 1980-81; embraces a study of UN resolutions, legal and human rights questions, land and water resources, Israeli settlements in the Occupied Territories and international perspectives on Palestinian rights; informative, pro-Palestinian.

Allen, Richard H.S. Imperialism and Nationalism in the Fertile Crescent: Sources and Prospects of the Arab Israeli Conflict. New York & Toronto: Oxford Univ. Press, 1977, repr. 1977. 686 p. pap.

Traces the historical background, Judaic, Christian and Muslim, the birth of Zionism, the Mandate period, the creation of Israel, the first four Arab-Israeli Wars (that of 1973 in an Epilogue), and international repercussions; chronology, bibliography, maps.

El-Asmar, Fouzi. <u>To be an Arab in Israel</u>. Beirut: Institute for Palestine Studies, 1978. 247 p. $6.00 pap.

 A personal account of the author's life, from the occupation of Lydda, his hometown, by the Israelis in 1948, his life as a student, writer, poet and publisher; details his cooperation with Israelis in the peace movement, his arrests and the inhuman treatment he suffered over 15 months in Israeli prisons, followed by a year of house arrest, all without trial.

Buber, Martin. <u>A Land of Two Peoples: Martin Buber on Jews and Arabs</u>. Ed. with commentary by Paul R. Mendes-Fohr. New York & Toronto: Oxford Univ. Press, 1983. 320 p. $11.95 pap.

 Buber, a product of religious socialism, believed in the necessary relation between ethics and politics; defended the idea of Zionism but opposed its implementation by force, holding the ideal of equal rights for both Arabs and Jews.

Burns, General E.L.M. <u>Between Arab and Israeli</u>. Washington, D.C.: Institute for Palestine Studies, 1969 (repr. of 1962 ed.). 336 p. $12.95.

 A classic by a famous Canadian who was appointed Commander of the UN Emergency Force following the Six Day War of June, 1967: a factual account of the work of the UN force, its problems and violations of the armistice; interesting and authoritative.

Davis, Uri and N. Megvinsky. <u>Documents from Israel: Readings for a Critique of Zionism, 1967-73</u>. London: Ithaca, 1975. 228 p. £2.80 pap.

 A collection of articles by two Jewish authors, translated from the Hebrew press and official documents; begins with the Israeli Law of Return aimed at creating an exclusively Jewish state, moving on to chapters dealing with Land and Land Policies, official attitudes toward the Arab population and the application of Israeli discriminatory policies.

Forrest, A.C. The Unholy Land. Toronto: McClelland and Stewart, 1971. 173 p.

A moving first hand account of the Palestinians, both the refugees outside and those who remain within Israel and the Occupied Territories, and also a powerful indictment of Israel's treatment of them. Forrest was a Canadian United Church minister and journalist who had formerly been "pro-Israeli" and "mildly anti-Arab"; a plea for enlightened action to procure a just peace and security for both sides.

Halabi, Emile. The Secret Life of Saeed, the Ill-fated Pessoptimist. New York: Vantage Press, 1982. 169 p. $8.95.

The author, a former member of the Knesset, is one of the most highly regarded Palestinian writers and journalists in Israel. Saeed, the picaresque, tragi-comic hero of the story, is an informer for the Zionist State, but his stupidity, candor and cowardice make him more of a victim than a villain. Through Saeed's exploits, Emile Halabi reveals the hardships and struggles of the Arabs in Israel.

Halsell, Grace. Journey to Jerusalem. New York: Macmillan Publishing Co., 1981. 193 p. pap.

A very personal account of the Arab/Israeli conflict, with an emphasis on the plight of Palestinians living under occupation. Through dialogue, the author allows Palestinians to describe their daily lives and experiences under occupation and, in the process, shows the incongruity between the existing conflicts and the dictates of the three world religions which emerged in that region.

Harkabi, Yehoshafat. Israel's Fateful Hour. New York: Harper & Row, 1988. 256 p.

Written by the former Chief of Israeli intelligence, former advisor to Monachem Begin and a leading authority on the Arab-Israeli conflict, the author argues that the status quo could lead to 'national suicide', that Israel confronts only two alternatives: 1) the acceptance of a Palestinian state, and 2) a Greater Israel. He argues that if Israel opts for a Greater Israel, the country will turn into a police state in which the Palestinians will become a majority ruled by a Jewish minority. He therefore opts for a Palestinian state on the West Bank and in Gaza.

Keller, Adam. Terrible Days: Social Divisions and Political Paradoxes in Israel. Amstelveen, Holland: Cypres, 1987. 200 p. pap.

A peace activist focuses on the paradoxes between parliamentary democracy in Israel, though "flawed", and autocratic rule in the Occupied Territories; examines anomalies in economic, political, social, religious and civil rights areas; ends with an account of the Peace Now movement and the 1982 Shatila and Sabra massacres.

Khalifeh, Sahar. (Translated by Trevor LeGossik). Wild Thorns. London: Al Saqi Books, 1985. 207 p.

A powerful account of life in the West Bank under Israeli occupation. The book delineates the conflict of a Palestinian returning to the area after several years of absence, the class struggle within the West Bank society, as well as the conflict of changing social values.

Moore, J.N., ed. The Arab-Israeli Conflict: Readings and Documents. New Jersey: Princeton Univ. Press, 1977. 1285 p. pap.

A comprehensive, judicious and balanced choice of documents and viewpoints on this intractable conflict, embracing the underlying issues, the first four Arab-Israeli Wars, the role of the U.N. and settlement proposals down to 1975; an indispensable research tool.

Nijim, Basheer K., ed. American Church Politics and the Middle East. Belmont, Mass.: Assoc. of Arab-American Univ. Graduates, 1982. 156 p. pap.

A valuable collection of articles surveying attitudes toward the Palestinian-Israeli question from Roman Catholicism to fundamentalism, plus a good discussion of Judaism vs. Zionism by Rabbi Elmer Berger; deals with such topics as the place of land in the religious contest, church politics and economics, and the influence of Christian Zionism on American policy in the Mid-East.

Palumbo, Michael. The Palestinian Catastrophe: the 1948 Expulsion of a People from their Homeland. London/Boston: Faber & Faber, 1987. 233 p. $29.95.

A carefully documented account of the forcible expulsion of the Palestinians, exploding the myth of the responsibility of Arab leaders for the mass exodus; recounts various massacres, of which Deir Yassin was only the most brutal, and the seizure of Palestinian property.

Quandt, Wm., Fuad Jabber and Ann M. Lesch. The Politics of Palestinian Nationalism. Berkeley: Univ. of Calif. Press, 1973. 234 p. $2.95 pap.

An examination of Palestinian nationalism: Part I on the Mandate period, by Ann Lesch; Part II, dealing with the post-1967 development of the movement, by Quandt; with Part III, by Fuad Jabber, concentrating on its relationship with inter-Arab politics, culminating in Black September in Jordan in 1970.

Shehadeh, Raja. Samed: Journal of A West Bank Palestinian. New York: Adama Books, 1984. 143 p. pap.

'Samid' is one who perseveres, who remains steadfast. This journal by a West Bank lawyer who founded and is the co-director of Law in the Service of Man, a human rights organization, documents the feelings, thoughts, aspirations and hopes of a thoughtful and peace-loving Palestinian as he attempts to endure and deal with the fact of occupation. A very personal account, touching and easily readable.

Shipler, David K. Arab and Jew: Wounded Spirits in a Promised Land. New York: Penguin, 1987, repr. of Random House 1986 ed. 596 p. $10.95 pap.

A study of forces producing hatred, i.e. war, nationalism, terrorism and religion; of images and stereotypes held by both Arabs and Jews of each other; and of the complexity of interaction between the few Jews and Arabs actively searching for reconciliation; makes the presumption of equal rights based on equally valid historical claims and nationalisms on both sides, without dealing with the basic

151

injustice of the dispossession of the Palestinians; of interest as an attempt at a non-judgmental position.

Al-Udhari, Abdullah (Translator). Victims of a Map. London: Al Saqi Books, 1984. 165 p. pap.
    A bilingual anthology of Arabic poetry including the works of two Palestinian poets, Mahmud Darwish and Samih al-Qasim, and the Syrian/Lebanese poet, Adonis.

Zureik, Elia. The Palestinians in Israel: a Study in Internal Colonialism. London/Boston: Routledge & Kegan Paul, 1979. 249 p. £8.50.
    A carefully researched study of the Israeli "internal colonialism" of its Arab minority, documented in the proletarization of the peasantry through exclusivist labour policies and the expropriation of their land, in the institutionalization of political, economic and social control, and the co-opting of Palestinian professionals; sees the only hope for a resolution of their situation in an intensification of the struggle for self-determination.

A NOTE ON CONTRIBUTORS

Dr. Mahmoud Ayoub
Professor of Comparative Religion and Islam, Department of Religion, Temple University; a practicing Muslim and one of North America's leading authorities on Islam and Muslim-Christian relations.

Prof. Issa J. Boullata
Professor of Arabic Literature and Language at McGill University's Institute of Islamic Studies, and has written extensively on Modern Arabic Literature

Mr. Naji Farah
A Canadian of Palestinian origin, formerly principal of a Palestinian high school in Shefa-Amr, and presently Information Officer of the Canadian Palestine Association.

Prof. James A. Graff
Professor of Philosophy at the University of Toronto, and President of the Near East Cultural Foundation of Canada.

Mr. Sami Hadawi
A distinguished Palestinian who worked under the British Mandate Government; author of many well-known books and articles on the Palestinian Question.

Prof. Lorne M. Kenny
Professor Emeritus and former Chairman of the Department of Middle East and Islamic Studies, University of Toronto; Chairman of the Board of the Near East Cultural and Educational Foundation of Canada.

Prof. Peyton Lyon
Professor Emeritus, Department of Political Science, Carleton University and an authority on Canada's role in the UN.

Prof. Fouad Moughrabi
Professor of Political Science at the University of Tennessee, Chatanooga, Tennessee and an authority on the politics of the Middle East and on public opinion relevant to Middle East issues.

Dr. Farid Ohan
Teaching-Master of Philosophy and Psychology, Seneca College of Applied Arts and Technology, and Vice-President of the Near East Cultural and Educational Foundation of Canada.

Mr. Habib Salloum
Author of numerous articles on the Arab World, Past President and co-founder of the Canadian Arab Friendship Society of Toronto, the oldest Canadian Arab society in the city.

Prof. Ghada Talhami
Assistant Professor of Politics, specializing in the Middle East and Africa, at Lake Forest College, Lake Forest, Illinois, U.S.A.

Mr. Ken Tancock
Retired History teacher and former head of the History Department at Sir Wilfred Laurier Collegiate Institute, Scarborough, Ontario.

Prof. Elia Zureik
Professor of Sociology, Queen's University, one of the leading international authorities on the Palestinians and Publications Director of the Near East Cultural and Educational Foundation of Canada.